Inaugural Gall II

The Audacity Continues

Inaugural Gall II

The Audacity Continues

By Lara Mars

ISBN 978-0-9855518-2-7

Half Century Publishing LLC.

Toms River, New Jersey 08755

The information written and provided in this book is believed to be true to the best of my knowledge. If any statements are subject to controversy based on my own opinions they are protected by the First Amendment and free speech provisions in the U.S. Constitution.

Dedicated

To My Lord and Savior

Jesus Christ

Comforter, Counselor, Teacher

and

To My Dad who Mirrored this Example

To My Family

And Every Patriotic American

Voting to Save America

Make America Great Again

"Freedom is never more than one generation away from extinction. We didn't pass it to our children in the bloodstream. It must be fought for, protected, and handed on for them to do the same, or one day we will spend our sunset years telling our children and our children's children what it was once like in the United States where men were free."

— Ronald Reagan

Table of Contents

"The only thing more dangerous than ignorance is arrogance."

—Albert Einstein

Prologue

America is in a crisis mode. Never before have we been so divided. Since Covid 19 Americans are willing to completely negate, cancel, or disregard anyone including family members who do not agree with them on every issue.

Many feel frustrated, betrayed, and powerless because they believe the country is in a forced decline induced by the Biden /Harris administration and certain government agencies.

Some of the leadership in these government agencies have gone rogue with unchecked power and are subjecting Americans to decisions contrary to the will of "We the People."

Our elected state representatives have not restricted or removed the authority from these unelected government leaders, who I believe are complicit in the managed decline of America.

In fact, representatives, both Democrats and Republicans have not addressed the people's deepest concerns.

Political parties are now bought and paid for by global elitists betting on a nations rise or fall according to their financial gains.

Most news media outlets are also being weaponized to misinform and divide us.

If this continues, America will be without power, without financial means, without borders, and without a global influence.

I hope you will join the effort to save America, along with others joining us like Robert F. Kennedy Jr. and Tulsi Gabbard.

Then the New Republican Party, Conservative Democrats, and Smart Independents will unite together to make America Healthy, Safe, and Great Again.

I hope that 2024 will bring renewal and rebirth for freedom and hope in America.

Chapter One

The only thing necessary for the triumph of evil is for good men to do nothing.

Edmund Burke

Political Unrest

Cause and Effect

Under President Obama we saw America's leadership in the world begin to decline. The country became divided along racial and economic lines. The Department of Justice (DOJ) was bastardized under his leadership, and big tech corporations slipped into bed with the government.
https://www.technologyreview.com/2017/01/09/154678/obamas-technology-legacy/

Secretary of State Hillary Clinton was investigated by the FBI so the agency would appear to be nonpartisan. She was never charged for keeping an unsecure server with classified information in an unsecure location or for destroying evidence and deleting emails.
https://www.foxnews.com/transcript/did-clinton-destroy-evidence-during-email-investigation

More importantly there was no accountability for the brave lives lost or the lies told to the American people with regard to the attack at Benghazi.
https://www.politico.com/blogs/under-the-radar/2017/05/26/hillary-clinton-benghazi-email-suits-dismissed238880#:~:text=Suit%20against%20Hillary%20Clinton%20over%20Benghazi%20deaths%20

Others would have been indicted for far less. Were we surprised? This was now the new normal.

Then at the end of Obamas second term our government agencies decided they would take control of the 2016 Trump vs. Clinton Presidential election. This was demonstrated by Peter Strzok the Deputy Assistant Director of the FBI's Counter intelligence Division, as he confided in his co-worker Lisa Page to not worry that there was an "insurance policy" should Trump actually win the election.
https://www.washingtonpost.com/politics/2019/03/14/what-strzok-page-insurance-policy-text-was-actually-about/

Mr. Strzok also led the investigation on President elect Trump's campaign with regards to the "Russian interference" during the 2016 Presidential election, but no one expected the magnitude of gall that was to come from these once trusted agencies.

To create false allegations against the Republican President Elect, and then to continue treasonous lies against a then sitting President was unprecedented. Yet many government officials took part in this disloyalty without consequences.

Though they were unsuccessful to prevent Trump's 2016 victory, the harassment continued throughout President Trump's four-year term in office.

Why? Because President Trump was the first President in a long while that the "Deep State" was unable to buy or control. In other words, he was a threat to their unelected power. This is what Democrats mean when they refer to "Our Democracy."

Our so called "Democracy" consists of their unchecked power and keeping it all status quo. Every level of government seems to have its own goals and agendas and are starting to function as if they are no longer subject to the will of "We the People." This ideology runs deeper and wider than we ever imagined. Over time it has created a pseudo shadow government many call the Deep State.

The Deep State represents the many layers and levels of government and government agencies which remain the same with each passing election. The State Department is only one of them. It consists of many sub-agencies that have seen presidents come and go for many years.

The State Dept is run by the Secretary of State and consists of Foreign Service, Civil Service, and the U.S. Agency for International Development aka USAID. USAID gives more unregulated aid and funding around the world in addition to all the money sent to the United Nations. USAID has its own global and green agenda, all paid for with U.S. tax dollars.

*USAID has been dismantled by President Trump and the remnants are now being overseen by the Secretary of State Marco Rubio. This will preserve our nation's wealth and reputation around the globe for decades to come. Thia may also produce enemies who are corrupt and dependent on this out flow of unregulated funds.

Most government agencies are housed by left leaning liberal graduates from some of the most prestigious colleges throughout the country. Colleges that have, for decades, created a false narrative about America and America's place in the world.

False narratives of how unjust, prejudice, and unremarkable America is and was throughout history. They teach and encourage a self-loathing Anti-American sentiment and justify crimes against Americas free market capitalist system, and the U.S. Constitution. Promoting Socialism, and even Marxism, an egalitarian equal distribution, as a fairer more socially just system in its place. Failing to mention these Godless forms of controlled government have produced only poverty and death for millions of people around the world.

These institutes of "Higher Education" believe Globalization is the only answer for peace in the world. Most colleges also promote climate change like a foreboding religion, victimization of all minorities, and racism against all others as oppressors.

They produce anti-American graduates who then proceed to do the bidding of the elite green global social class. Some even influencing their parents who believe they must be smarter because of the exorbitant amount of money they spent on their education.

Then federal agencies employ and promote them over time to top-tier positions in almost every government sector. These once respected federal agencies have now gone rogue with unchecked power and have decided that they will take it from here in order to save our democracy.

The FBI, CIA, DHS, NIH, and others, all unelected, have their own agendas, far removed from their original mandated responsibilities; separate and apart from the will of the American people who pay their salaries.

The Biden Legacy

Biden has been representing the State of Delaware as a Senator since 1972. He has been in politics for over fifty years.

The Bidens now appear to be one of the most compromised political families in U.S. history. Democrats want us to believe that "hide in the basement" Biden really won the 2020 election and received more votes than Barack Obama did? https://www.politifact.com/article/2020/dec/15/how-biden-managed-win-far-more-votes-2020-obama-di/

The Democrat leaders in many failing blue state cities seem to get elected over and over again. Nancy Pelosi, while addressing Alexandria Ocasio-Cortez's re-election in NYC; said "A glass of water with a (D) in front of it can be elected in her district."

Why is that? Many local residents expressed great disappointment in AOC for the loss of many good Amazon jobs in Queens.

It's the same with Democrat Nancy Pelosi in San Francisco. She has represented her districts since 1988. With strong fundraising and liberal constituents, she remained in House to become undefeatable by common metrics. But her district has become one of the worst in California. Along with Kamala Harris, the rates of homelessness, drug addiction, and crimes have risen substantially on her watch over the years.

This leaves many to believe that voting in these blue states is more than just a repetitive coincidence, but that reelection is somewhat guaranteed. Leaders in these failed states remain in perpetuity without any challenges or questions asked election after election.

Many Americans believe most blue state elections are rigged. So, what if Democrats had enough time and the cover of the Covid 19 virus to steal a Presidential election?

I absolutely believe the 2020 election was stolen.

That is why President Trump assumed that VP Pence could somehow stop the questionable election certification. Like many of us, he believed it to be erroneous therefore it was invalid.

Unfortunately, President Trump misunderstood. All the contested states with Republican State Legislatures, and or Republican Governors could have stopped it by not certifying the results of their individual states if they believed it to be fraudulent.

But everything happens for a reason and a purpose which is revealed over time.

So Biden was declared the winner, and the Blue half of the country pretended not to know what happened. They willingly remained delusional because somehow their impotent candidate won. They didn't care to question how.

When the so-called January 6th incident happened, no matter how or why, it posed yet another opportunity for Democrats to pull a "Rahm" and "Never let a crisis go to waste," *as Rahm Emanuel, Obama's White House Chief of Staff once advised. Now they could wield yet another accusation against President Trump. They called it an "Insurrection."

The phony January 6th Committee was appointed by Democrats for Democrats with a few "never Trump" Republicans. They were all appointed by Pelosi, not Senate leader McConnell or House Speaker McCarthy. This was against all existing House precedent.

In my opinion, this invalidates any of their so-called findings to nothing more than the final attempt to keep President Trump from ever running again for the Presidency.

The Committee never called for defense witnesses, never considered all available facts, and information. They also prevented Capital video from being released because they knew just like the fake stories of Russian collusion, and the Ukrainian phone call, they were creating another false narrative in order to accomplish their ultimate goal; to undermine Trump and keep their political power intact.

Once again, the news media outlets were complicit in this charade against Americans. While covering for Biden, they failed to report all of the unfolding political corruption and financial accusations against then VP Joe Biden and his son, Hunter Biden.

Instead there was a constant drumbeat about a January 6th insurrection.

Many patriotic Americans have been sitting in jail since Jan 6, 2021. Their civil rights were being violated on a daily basis. Many were given the maximum sentence as a warning to all future Republican protestors.

https://www.axios.com/2023/09/01/jan-6-longest-sentences-list

In contrast to all the Black Lives Matter aka BLM and Defund the Police protestors who caused millions of dollars in damages, used violence against our police officers, many people died, and most protestors were set free. https://www.heritage.org/crime-and-justice/commentary/we-need-congressional-investigation-the-2020-riots

On January 6th, most patriots walked respectfully through the Capitol Building to express their dissent. Some were even waved in by police to enter the Capitol. One police officer escorted a group to where the House members had been gathered to certify the election results.

Out of hundreds of thousands of protestors, a few of them broke some windows. But the only person who died, was a veteran named Ashli Babbitt. She was a patriot trying to stop others from entering the doors to the House floor. She was unarmed, shot by a capital police officer who was never held to the same standard as police in other protests.

No police officers were killed on January 6th despite what the fake news was reporting.

19

Insurrection really? With no guns, very little damage, one patriot killed. I believe there were people planted in the crowd either to stir up trouble, or to incite violence, and maybe even commit the criminal acts we saw in an effort to achieve the optics desired.

Democrats wanted to portray patriotic Americans as violent insurrectionists and chill their free speech about the questionable election results.

The protesters were not trying to overturn the results of a legitimate election; they were trying to stop a Presidential election from being stolen in the midst of the Covid chaos.

The political and governmental leaders who remain in control are the danger to our Democratic Republic. They are drunk on keeping their power by any means necessary.

The outcome of the 2024 election will determine our survival and ultimately our destiny.

Election Interference -Again and Again

Evidence continues to confirm our government agencies are being weaponized not only by the Democrats against the American people, but also against their political opponents.

The DOJ appeared to be coordinating with local Democratic District Attorneys and Attorney General's to launch several Trump Investigations with the intent to indict him out of the 2024 election cycle. This is called "Lawfare," and it is unopposed in one party states and districts like New York, California, and Washington DC.

The first of many accusations against Trump was a criminal trial in April 2024. Using Democratic AG's and DA's, and partisan Democrat Judges, they would attempt to destroy his reputation and diminish his political viability.

This was purposeful since April was the beginning of the 2024 Presidential Election Season.
Eventually anyone and everyone connected to or fond of President Trump was a target of investigation.

This is the first time the Democrat Party used "Lawfare" against a political opponent. This was not the first time Democrats attempted to influence or subvert our elections.

Remember the FBI decided to spy on the Trump campaign in 2016. False evidence was submitted under the Foreign Intelligence Surveillance Act to federal courts to obtain warrants against members of Trump's campaign. While the American people were lied to continually via most news media organizations.

https://thehill.com/policy/national-security/474964-surveillance-court-accuses-fbi-agents-of-giving-misleading-basis-for/

In the 2020 Trump vs. Biden campaign the NY Post reported about fifty-one "spies" who were active CIA contractors who gave cover to VP Biden by claiming in writing that Hunter Biden's laptop was Russian disinformation.
https://nypost.com/2024/06/26/opinion/how-cia-interference-with-the-spies-who-lie-letter-made-biden-the-president/

Let's not forget all the social media censorship of conservative speech, and accounts were being cancelled or labeled misinformation. While the news media was covering for the Bidens.
https://www.heritage.org/technology/commentary/biden-administration-outsourcing-online-censorship-conservatives

Democrats were hard at work in 2020 convincing some moderate Republican leaders in Georgia and elsewhere to relax voting standards under the guise of Covid fears. Election laws were changed without the state legislative process. In other words, illegally.

Trump was well ahead on election night, but the media outlets refused to call the state of Georgia for Trump. Then the same thing happened in Pennsylvania, and Arizona, even though Trump held a handsome lead.

After counting all of the nefarious ballots and continuing the counting all night, Biden won. America was in disbelief. We suspected it and then we heard it, the truth out of Joe Bidens' own mouth, but the media dismissed it.

Joe Bidens Freudian Slip, …….

"We have put together, I think, the most extensive, and inclusive voter fraud organization in the history of American politics."
https://www.berksgop.com/biden-fraud-confession/

That's right, you said it Joe, a huge on the ground voter fraud organization…..

I'm sure all the usual players were there. Every neighborhood community organization, aka Democratic on the ground operation.

There was also the social media icon giving Democrats large donations and supplying convenient drop boxes in blue states. While he simultaneously censored so called

"misinformation" on his social media platform. It's
criminal because it's election interference.
https://nypost.com/2024/08/27/us-news/mark-
zuckerberg-admits-biden-admin-pressured-facebook-to-
censor-covid-content-says-it-was-wrong-to-suppress-
hunter-laptop-coverage/

There are also many statistical anomalies that cannot be
explained away. For example President Trump received
10.1 million more votes than he did in the 2016 election.
More than any other sitting president in history.
https://www.nytimes.com/interactive/2020/11/16/us/polit
ics/election-turnout.html

House Republicans who ran for office won all 27 out of
27 races. Biden lost both Ohio and Florida even though
the polls said he was leading.

Trump won 51 out of 57 Bellwether counties that have
determined the President since the year 2000. There are
many other anomalies. Please search the link to see all
the information available.
https://www.leelanau.gov/downloads/b_wiesner_041820
23.pdf
Let's not forget over 140 sworn affidavits signed under
the penalty of perjury. All attesting to the election day
irregularities. From voting centers removing Republican

oversight, to covering up the windows with paper to prevent poll workers from even viewing the count.

In Georgia, there were allegations of flooding so they could shut down the counting center. Republicans poll watchers were sent home. Democrats were unaware of the cameras recording all of the suitcases of ballots being rolled out from under covered tables and put through the counting machines over and over, and over again. All said to be marked for Biden. We all saw it; there's no need to deny it.

Election officials in Fulton County Georgia first said a pipe burst in a room of the State Farm Arena where absentee ballots were being held, then later they said it was a leaky toilet.
(https://www.foxnews.com/politics/georgia-investigating-vote-counting-delayed-by-flooding-in-democratic-county-gop-poll-watchers-told-counting)

Many printed articles and media news organizations backed these allegations without question. Which, once again, gave cover to many false Democratic statements.
https://www.politico.com/news/2020/11/03/burst-pipe-delays-atlanta-absentee-vote-433988

https://abcnews.go.com/Politics/pipe-bursts-atlanta-arena-causing-hour-delay-processing/story?id=73981348

In Michigan, poll watchers testified of trucks disguised as food vendors with no food dropping off boxes of ballots. Showing up all hours throughout the late night, with only one pick on the entire ballot: Joe Biden.

Below is an excerpt from what CNN at the time called misinformation, yes now we know better…

(https://www.cnn.com/business/live-news/election-2020-misinformation)

"What they swear to, is that at 4:30 in the morning a truck pulled up to the Detroit center where they were counting ballots. The people thought it was food, so they all ran to the truck. It wasn't food. It was thousands and thousands of ballots," said former Mayor Rudy Giuliani.

In a ruling on November 13, 2020, Judge Timothy Kenny of the Third Judicial Circuit Court of Michigan invalidated the affidavits Mr. Giuliani referenced. The judge ruled that the claims regarding the nature and quantity of the ballots were speculations at best and sinister at worst.

" *The Michigan judge ruled that such affidavits claiming widespread voter fraud were baseless.* " That's not fact, it's only his opinion, and because he is a judge he willed it to be so.

There were also mail in ballots received after the legal date allowed, being forwarded, and counted under Post

Office Supervisor's instructions. Shameless acts of voting fraud, and no one held accountable. https://www.projectveritas.com/news/anonymous-usps-coraopolis-pa

Late ballots were set aside, again, and stamped with corrected dates so they could be counted in Michigan. https://www.projectveritas.com/news/anonymous-usps-traverse-city-michigan

This took some time to gather but thank you to Judicial Watch. I hope some eyes will be opened now.

How about states that had more votes than voters?

According to Judicial Watch there were 353 counties in 29 states that had voter registration rates exceeding (100%) one hundred percent. This amounted to 1.8 million more registered voters than eligible voting aged citizens. https://www.judicialwatch.org/new-jw-study-voter-registration/

1.8 million more votes than voters, and all of these multi-state violations put together caused basement Biden to beat the best President since Ronald Reagan.

So why did the Supreme Court deny hearing the cases of voter fraud in all of the contested battleground states? Because ultimately it was not up to SCOTUS, it was up to the individual states.

If the Supreme Court had uncertified the certified election, it would have set a dangerous precedent for all future elections. Then every legally certified election could now be contested, it would have insured a future of chaos and anarchy.

President Trump's lawyers were well aware of the voter fraud. So they sent out teams of lawyers to each contested state. They sat before state assemblies and explained for days, as we watched on television, that if the state assemblies believed the election was incorrect and there was no way to correct it; they were obligated to not certify the state election. This was their job.

Meanwhile all summer long prior to the election we watched the violence from the George Floyd riots and the "defund the police" movements. As well as the Black Lives Matter movements, and the crime sprees caused by no bail district attorneys which emboldened smash and grab mobs.

All this was happening in the months leading up to, and even after the 2020 Presidential election. The riots and the unrest was meant to instill fear into everyday people. In my opinion, the unrest and violence was privately funded by non-profit cohorts in order to undermine our nations stability.

Concerns of retaliatory acts of violence were not hard to imagine, had the state assemblies not certified the election. The Pennsylvania state assembly vowed they would do all they could to stop the travesty of election fraud. Then proceeded to certified the 2020 election results anyway.

Continued Election Misinformation

After the stolen 2020 election, in my opinion, Americans were the victims of government and news media disinformation for the next several years.

Since then the news media outlets have continued to suppress legitimate stories that would have exposed the compromised Biden administration and various members of the Biden family.

Perhaps that was the higher purpose of the stolen election: to expose the years of Joe Bidens political corruption and to begin the dismantling of his political and financial empire.

Unless Joe Biden became President, we would not have known about the families, more than twenty shell companies, alleged foreign payoffs, and tactics of the Biden family brand of business.

The Biden family and their business associates, as well as their companies received over ten million dollars from foreign nationals as the records show. The payments occurred while Biden was Vice President, and also after his time in office ended, as reported by the National Review.
https://www.nationalreview.com/news/bidens-used-web-of-shell-companies-to-conceal-foreign-cash-bank-records-obtained-by-house-gop-reveal/

Broken Promises and Lies

The midterm elections of 2022 also proved to be very disappointing. Let's put aside ballot box stuffing and nursing home(s) ballot harvesting that preceded in the 2020 election for just a moment. I'm sure that also happened in 2022.

But the Democrats have become such experts at deception now we just expect a measure of this bu@#sh*t in every election cycle.

The Democrats, in an attempt to bribe the millennials in 2022, promised to pay off student loan debt. Whether it was a good idea or not, it caused a greater youth turnout for Democrats than Republicans.

Democrats, again with the complicity of the news media outlets, also scared women into believing that abortion would somehow return to the back allies. Even though after the overturn of Roe v Wade, abortion is still legal in many mostly blue states.

News media outlets continue to spread the same disinformation as they continue to accuse Conservatives of doing exactly what the Democrats are doing.

Rush Limbaugh always said….**" If you want to know what the Democrats are up to, just listen to what they are accusing us of doing…."**

Half the country is ignorant of what is happening simply because the fake news media outlets are refusing to report the news accurately. Many people don't know truth from lies, for the most part we believe what is said on television. Which begs the question; why aren't licensed broadcast companies held responsible for disseminating disinformation?

Enemies Foreign and Domestic

FBI whistle blowers came forth to testify before congress that the agency had abandoned the normal protocols relating to January 6th in an attempt to inflate the numbers for domestic violence.

This was done by individually labeling each name as a separate file in order to increase the appearance of domestic terrorism among regular Americans, making it seem more prevalent.

https://www.americanpress.com/2023/05/18/breaking-whistleblower-says-fbi-manipulated-jan-6-cases-to-make-domestic-terrorism-appear-widespread/

The Department of Justice also tried to label concerned parents as domestic terrorists. If parents attended a school board meeting and expressed their frustration about dangerous curricular being taught to their children, school board members needed only to say they felt threatened or afraid and parents could be charged with a crime.

https://judiciary.house.gov/media/press-releases/us-house-judiciary-republicans-doj-labeled-dozens-of-parents-as-terrorist

This is another example of chilling free speech. If law abiding citizens try to invoke their rights, they are intimidated into thinking they are doing something wrong and are bullied into silence.

Since President Obama's administration, the deep state has coerced big tech, and most of the news media outlets into compliance. In my opinion, they have all assisted in destroying our free speech, our free and fair elections, and are actively destroying our Democratic Republic.

We are not a Democracy; we are a Democratic Republic. We vote in elections and are governed by laws, and our rights are outlined in the U.S. Constitution.

Since 2021 the Democrats have not protected our borders. They are bankrupting our nation with reckless spending and are putting the U.S. in danger by not guarding against foreign aggressors, namely China, N. Korea, Russia, and Iran.

We must protect our freedoms, and our sovereignty. We should not allow those who do not wish to truly assimilate to come into America. Especially when their ideologies cannot coexist with our Constitution, laws, or values. They should not become U.S. citizens.

The 1992 house decision for foreign born naturalized citizens to hold any high public office should be reversed; due to national security risks, and questionable loyalties.

Today in America patriots are called criminals. Criminals are called victims. Police are called racists, while brutal criminals roam free. Conservative Americans are called MAGA extremists. Christians are called intolerant because they don't want drag queens to teach or influence their children.

Over a decade ago, I warned that our real enemies are domestic. These enemies are sitting in agencies of power. Many in high positions with tremendous influence caused the erosion we are experiencing today.

Globalists, Communists, Socialists, Marxists, and Green purveyors influence our leaders, who believe they know better, and that the end will justify their means. Even if they have to dismantle America to achieve it.

Why? In order to commit to or create a true global one world economy, or a global reset, or a new world order, globalists must drastically reduce or remove America's standing in the world.

Western Europe is also being overwhelmed by mass immigration of foreign nationals as well in order to undermine their wealth and security.

Can you see it now? Our problems are all self-inflicted by a common agenda propagated by our domestic enemies to keep us divided, and in need of an ever increasing government.

Others, perhaps like Barack and Michelle Obama, and maybe some BLM members may think we deserve this. That is rightful retribution for the wrongs of the past like slavery.

So then all of our self-corrections over the years doesn't absolve any of the past wrongs?

Obama being President doesn't absolve any of our so-called prejudices. So what will? The people who never owned slaves must now pay people who were never slaves some amount of money in reparations. This has already been proposed in California.
https://www.washingtonpost.com/nation/2024/06/28/reparations-california-budget/

Half of the country is politically unaware, and it feels like we are one election away from no longer being the United States of America. Conservatives are not law-breaking people and hopefully we can right this wrong course for our nations survival in the 2024 election.

The Battle Rages On

With every passing year the audacity increases. Our side is completely unaware as to how low the opposition will go. Believe me, ballots are probably being rigged all year long, but we don't think that way.

America needs to be saved from all treasonous traitors. How bad is it when you can say you are a Socialist or Marxist and we don't deport you out of the country? Yes, freedom of speech, say what you want but we don't have to let you stay here if you abhor, harm, and undermine America.

Politicians who repeatedly lie to the American people should be barred from reelection. (D)Adam Schiff was cheered on by his Democratic cohorts in the halls of congress as he was censured by the 118th Congress for repeatedly misleading the American people with false claims of proof of Trump/ Russia collusion. https://www.foxnews.com/politics/adam-schiff-censured-house-false-allegations-trump-russia-collusion

Government employees like Dr. Anthony Fauci, who make false claims and lie to the American people should lose their jobs and their pensions.

He gave misinformation to the American people on more than one occasion. Wear a mask, don't wear a mask. Get a vaccine, then get a booster. Get four vaccines, and you still catch Covid.

More importantly all the misinformation given with regard to the origins of the Covid 19 virus, the next chapter will explain in more detail.

This was unacceptable and intolerable.

Let's not forget we were locked down and censored, lied to and overwhelmed with fear. Many Americans died and they died alone during Covid 19 due to the medical misinformation and disinformation we received.

Let's never forget, and if possible, let's hold them all accountable.

Is America Becoming a Police State

Are we leaving a free America to the next generation?

Orwell's novel 1984 describes Britain under the totalitarian Oceanian regime that continuously invokes and helps to cause a war in perpetuity. This war is then used as a reason for subjecting the people to surveillance by Big Brother and invasive police searches. Sounds somewhat familiar.
https://en.wikipedia.org/wiki/Police_state

In my first book, Inaugural Gall: The Audacity of Liberals, I said America was being used as the police of the entire world. We sacrificed and fought for what we believed to be just causes. Over time and especially under Democrat Administrations our military has become abused and forgotten.
We receive nothing in return for our blood and sacrifices. Now America is becoming war weary.

What are the Characteristics of a "Police State?" I believe they are as follows:

Increasing regulations over the general population. On every level especially with regards to the false narrative of global warming issues to instill fear and gain control of manufacturing, production, and output. With increased "use" taxes on the population.

- Government partnership with big tech and telecommunications corporations for surveillance purposes. Look up and you'll see cameras on every corner and stop light. We should have no crime at all, but unfortunately that's not the case. We are watched continually as criminals are set free.

- Government of the ruling party's use of "lawfare" to attack political opponents.

- Government control of energy usage and production / or lack of energy production to increase inflation and increase product costs. Causing the middle class to pay more for everything.

My overall suspicion is financial elites and globalists are trying to decimate our wealth and independence by financially ruining the US economy. Our current leaders are shrinking the middle class into poverty by overspending and printing of more money.

- Government and State mandates counting illegals in the census population not outlined in the US or State Constitutions.

- Government with One-party influence over most media information and misinformation w/o credible checks. Nor any consequences for fabrications and or disinformation to Americans.

- One party influence over two or more large states like California and New York State Assemblies creating poverty, drug addiction, and increases in crime. This creates dependence on the state and local governments. These States then receive greater financial support for failing cities and sanctuary city status.

- Government and State controls of education pushing historical propaganda. Universities receiving public tax dollars. Which are ultimately used to undermine America by pushing Anti-American, and Anti-Capitalism. Encouraging students to engage in protests against the founding principles of our country such as free speech, faith, and family.

- State Control by increasing taxes and tolls preventing free movement from state-to-state w/o penalty, fees, or charges. The tolls in many states and bridges have become prohibitive forcing some people to refrain from free travel. I believe this is unconstitutional; we should have the "Freedom of Movement" from state to state as outlined in Article IV.

- Instead we have electronic punitive tolls and monitoring of everyone's everyday travel or commute.
  https://en.wikipedia.org/wiki/Police_state

- Any form of government consolidation or consolidation of financial services, communications, and information or a cancelling, or limiting of choices for these services.

- Any government or "One party" attempt to undermine or redefine the US Supreme Court or the U.S. Constitution or it's protections.

- Any government or "One party" attempt to undermine our sovereignty, induce chaos to impose a national emergency, military protocols, or curfews, or to temporarily suspend elections.

Today we are not considered a police state, but many of the regulations already exist.

Thank God we depend on His divine protections, and also the US Constitution because it is a brilliant masterpiece.

We must not allow the tyranny of a few to overwhelm us into believing they are the majority because they are not.

Chapter Two
<u>Dress Rehearsal For Global Control</u>

<u>Coronavirus Crisis</u>

Covid 19 Virus arrived in America the later part of 2019 but was officially announced in January 2020. It was actually the third virus to come from China. It was common sense this was biological warfare from the Wuhan lab; no one had to tell me that.

Why would China do that?

Because our U.S. economy was strong, our borders were secure, we were energy independent for the first time in my life, and China was not.

This was not the first time China used a virus. First it was H5N1, aka the bird flu, from Southern China.
https://www.sciencebuzz.org/blog/swine-flu-vs-bird-flu

Then there was H1N1 the swine flu. Although the World Health Organization said it originated in Mexico. The

WHO is a puppet for China, so I'm not sure I readily believe them.

Even so, the swine flu is very dangerous, and as reported by CNN in 2020, China has "discovered" a new swine flu that can potentially effect humans and cause a future pandemic.
https://www.cnn.com/2020/06/30/asia/china-swine-flu-pandemic-intl-hnk-scli-scn/index.html

After a considerable amount of time we learned that the U.S. generously funded the "gain of function research" on China's soil. Why would the U.S. finance a virus to be harmful to human beings, especially with such an aggressive adversary. It's unconscionable.

The National Institute of Health funded the gain of function research at the Wuhan lab in China through several award disbursements. The first was paid directly to the Wuhan University. The second award recipient was a company called EcoHealth Alliance. EcoHealth then gave directly to the Wuhan University and the Wuhan Institute of Virology.

The University of California Irvine was the third award recipient to funnel funding directly to the Wuhan Institute of Virology according to the Government Accountability Office (GAO-23-106119, pg.2) in a

report to congressional requests.
https://www.gao.gov/assets/gao-23-106119.pdf

Then there was the award from U.S. Agency for International Development aka USAID which gave funds through the University of California Davis, which gave funds to EcoHealth Alliance.

EcoHealth Alliance in turn gave funds to both the University of Wuhan and the Wuhan Institute of Virology. https://www.gao.gov/assets/gao-23-106119.pdf

The Government Accountability Office said the first three selected recipients received two hundred thousand dollars in direct awards from NIH. But all together these entities received over two hundred million dollars from federal award recipients and subrecipients.
https://www.gao.gov/assets/gao-23-106119.pdf

That is why China originally said the U.S. was responsible for Covid. So they were not completely wrong.

Covid Scare and Control of the Masses

This was a perfect opportunity for testing America's cooperation under synchronized global control mechanisms. Purported all over the world, some areas were held under the mandates of this auspicious catastrophe longer than others.

Our top-tier medical experts would report covid cases daily on a 24/7 news cycle. The result was that the nation was paralyzed with fear and uncertainty.

Here at home our "experts" persuaded then President Trump, against his better judgement, to shut down the U.S. economy. Our Democratic Congress proceeded to spend us into oblivion. Other lawmakers shut down schools but continued paying everyone and giving repeated stimulus payments to teachers to remain home.

Lawmakers agreed to disburse stimulus payments of $600 a week. In addition to a federal unemployment benefit of $300 a week for eleven weeks.
https://www.nytimes.com/article/stimulus-deal-update.html

Democrats did not worry about accountability because as usual the media would cover for them. The HHS will keep the population under control through fear and intimidation. Just give Americans some free cable movies and they will be content, for a while.

https://www.newsweek.com/here-are-networks-who-are-releasing-free-content-due-coronavirus-pandemic-1496073

Churches and schools would be closed, while liquor stores and abortion centers would remain open.

It's the closest to martial law and socialism in America I have ever seen. The stress took its toll, as worldwide domestic violence, drinking, and drug abuse soared. https://time.com/5928539/domestic-violence-covid-19/

Under Trump the vaccine development called "Operation Warp Speed" was implemented.

Trump is a businessman, not a politician, scientist, or doctor. He was surrounded by his so-called experts, namely Dr. Anthony Fauci, and Deborah Birx from the CDC and NIH. President Trump relied on their expertise to guide us through this unprecedented time.

VP Pence took the lead of the Covid task force. I think he did a very good job overall. Then Dr. Fauci began to undermine the confidence in the Trump / Pence leadership. Wear masks, don't wear masks, get vaccinated, get one, no two, but you can still get and transmit the virus.

It was also reported that Dr. Fauci may have tried to influence the CIA's investigation on the origins of the Covid 19 Virus. That is because he was indirectly involved with the gain of function research funding but repeatedly said that the virus came from the Hunan wet market. When in fact he knew it had originated at the Wuhan Virology lab. There is still no accountability from Dr. Fauci or by the upper echelons in the state health organizations.

For Americans suffering from the loss of this deadly virus, there were no funerals for families who lost loved ones, no Thanksgiving or Christmas gatherings, no Sunday gatherings at places of worship. Schools were closed, while people were labeled essential or non-essential.

Yet at the same time you could riot in large groups if you were a defund the police or BLM protestor, or a college student rioting for a democrat cause.

No one had clear answers. But the big pharmaceuticals were planning on making billions. Vaccine mandates without having any responsibility. Basically we all agreed to receive this vaccine without knowing if or what harm it will cause in the future.

Like any virus it had to run its course. This one of course was different; it was made to be deadlier. We were being told everyone was dying, when in fact only the most vulnerable were, the elderly, the immune system compromised, and those who had severe preexisting conditions.

The news organizations like CNN, MSNBC, and even Fox Cable news continued the drum beat of Covid,

Covid, Covid. Anything and everything was Trump's fault. It was disgusting. They spewed misinformation to all of us for years again, and again not held accountable.

Government and Media were the main source of dissemination of misinformation, and disinformation while actively accusing real doctors and medical professionals of misinforming the public and threatening revocation of their medical licensing and censorship if they continued.

Facebook and Twitter cancelled people who were trying to get the truth out, because we were not in as much danger as they led us to believe.

Children were certainly not in as much danger as older seniors. Yet parents were lining up to vaccinate their children with an untested, unnecessary vaccine that could possibly change their DNA forever. We won't know for a very long time; maybe never.

The media helped enforce compliance through fear tactics. Example: They reported about two hundred children died of Covid. That information out of context would put fear in the heart of any parent. While in perspective, over 400 children that same year died from drowning. Are we going to outlaw swimming?
www.cdc.gov/drowning/facts/index.html

We have yet to see what, if anything, will be the consequences of these vaccines. Be advised we took a huge step backwards for freedom in America. We also put America's children, our future, at risk with an untested vaccine.

Health workers became overwhelmed, and healthcare systems became more draconian. Individuals were not allowed to see loved ones, confirm, or deny certain medical treatments, and for every Covid fatality the healthcare system received an increase of money.

People complained that loved ones who died were being labeled as fatalities from Covid 19. If they received Medicare or were uninsured the hospitals received up to 20% more per victim.
https://www.usatoday.com/story/news/factcheck/2020/0 4/24/fact-check-medicare-hospitals-paid-more-covid-19- patients-coronavirus/3000638001/

As the pandemic spread, thousands of people started to die. I believe many things, but for sure I believe the widespread use of Remdesivir increased the fatalities.

> "Kidney disorders as serious adverse drug reactions of Remdesivir in Coronavirus disease 2019…" As listed on the National Library of Medicine website.

(https://www.ncbi.nlm.nih.gov/pmc/articles/PMC7907730/)

It was said before you were placed on a respirator you said goodbye to your family if possible, because you probably would not survive.

Remdesivir causes kidney damage, and renal failure. I believe this contributed to the rise in Covid 19 fatalities reported.

They continued to push its use knowing full well Hydroxychloroquine fared far better in a patients recovery.
https://www.scielosp.org/article/csp/2021.v37n10/e00077721/

Meanwhile……Help was sent but not accepted….why?

Then President Trump sent out two huge, fully equipped hospital ships to deal with the volume of patients. New York and California did not use these medical ships. Trump sent the USNS Comfort to the east coast, and the USNS Mercy to the west coast.

Samaritan's Purse, an International Missions agency also set up a complete mobile medical hospital at the Jacob Javits Center, only to be ignored.

I believe had these resources been used many people would have survived and maybe the pandemic would have been staved off. But perhaps that may not have been the objective of some blue state leaders. I think their objective was three-fold.

One: to utilize a wide spread pandemic with many fatalities while implementing state-wide controls. Shutting everything down and setting the stage for opportunity for increased funds into Democratic state coffers through emergency Covid funding.

Two: Enriching the big donor pharmaceutical companies and those who were heavily invested in them, by pushing for only vaccines and boosters and not therapeutics.

National Institute of Health would not even consider other medications available like Hydroxychloroquine or Ivermectin. It was said this would have blocked the emergency approvals for the untested Covid 19 vaccines.

Three: This created opportunity for widespread fraud in the 2020 Presidential election by pushing mail in ballots. The outrageous health mandates that were implemented, and lock downs kept us isolated, while information was censored on both news media and social media platforms.

The people who did not take the vaccine were suddenly being blamed for spreading the virus. They were losing their jobs. Military and hospital personnel were being let go. Pilots were being fired. Today we know the shot didn't make the virus any better or worse.

When we began to reopen you were asked to show proof of the two-shot vaccine or you would be ostracized. You would not be able to go to the movies, eat in a restaurant, fly, or even drive to another state.

After risking their lives the very people who were the heroes through it all; our first responders and hospital workers, were then fired or let go if they refused the vaccine for any reason. Even for health and medical reasons.

In fact, after the 2020 election, President Biden started blaming the unvaccinated for the continued spread of the virus. While he allowed millions of unvaccinated illegal migrants to cross our border w/o vetting them or implementing any mandatory vaccinations. This lunacy continued under his administration.
https://cis.org/Mortensen/No-Vaccine-Mandate-Illegal-Aliens

Millions crossed our unprotected border from 2021 through 2024. Many of the migrant children and adult illegal migrants were not mandated to receive basic immunizations like TB, Measles, or Polio. https://www.verifythis.com/article/news/verify/immigration/routine-vaccination-asylum-seekers-migrants-refugees-united-states-border-immigration/536-5a1ddfab-70f0-4af9-a676-987cd8627d00

This put Americans at risk again for diseases already commuted by basic mandatory medical vaccines. Some illegal migrants did receive the Covid 19 vaccine. It's my understanding if refused they were tagged and monitored until title 42 was rescinded.

How Low will They Go?

When the Covid 19 virus was unleashed by China did elite Democrats want it to spread here? Think it's crazy? Is it so hard to believe the old adage "the enemy of my enemy is my friend."

Dr. Anthony Fauci was on the inside and a part of President Trump's administration. He was not a fan or a friend of Trump, and in my opinion he continually gave Americans false and misleading information.

Wasn't it VP Biden who repeatedly called President Trump a racist because he restricted the influx of people

who traveled in from China and Europe because of the Covid outbreak?
https://nypost.com/2020/10/22/did-joe-biden-actually-call-trump-xenophobic/

Wasn't it Speaker Nancy Pelosi who was urging everyone to come out to San Francisco's Chinatown as she visited the area to show support.
https://www.cbsnews.com/sanfrancisco/news/coronavirus-speaker-house-nancy-pelosi-tours-san-franciscos-chinatown/

Healthcare: Control the Information, Control the Masses

The Patient Protection and Affordable Care Act (Obamacare) passed in 2009 has given the government and the state agencies permission to control the healthcare information we receive, which drives the healthcare decisions we make.

In 2020 the National Institute of Health and the healthcare community took it a step further. Depending on who you listened to or believed, our healthcare information has been manipulated, or worse, purposefully controlled with misinformation.

When the Covid 19 Virus hit America at the end of 2019, and was identified in January of 2020, none of the hospitals were ready for a pandemic. Everyone was glued to the TV screen waiting to hear all of the information that was available.

We assumed the information we were receiving was the truth. Where it came from, how severe it was, who was most vulnerable, and what to do to avoid getting it.

We received none of that. We were told masks made no difference. Everyone was equally vulnerable. We were told the mortality rate was very high, and there were no drugs readily available to help it or cure it.

We were told it came from a Huanan seafood "wet market" in Wuhan China, and not from the Wuhan Institute of Virology, less than seven miles away.

We were lied to about many things. If I asked you which federal agency was in charge during the Covid Pandemic, you would probably say the CDC or NIH, right? Wrong.

Mr. Jeffery Tucker is the founder and President of the Brownstone Institute. He is the author of thousands of articles, and a columnist for the Epoch Times; one of only a few news sources I trust.

His *Epoch Times* article questioned Federal Emergency Management Agency's national alert to all cell phones on October 4, 2023. His concern was with regard to why this "emergency alert test" felt different, and why Americans should be aware of its implications.

While a government agency spokesperson said it was no different than the emergency broadcast systems of the past; his concern was that FEMA holds no elected official who voted to do this; but it was a decision by the "Administrative State;" which seems to be wielding exceedingly increasing authority over our freedoms.

Likewise, unbeknownst to many of us, FEMA was the agency in charge during Covid Pandemic, not the CDC or NIH as reported and we were led to believe.

In his article he referenced a Health and Human Services document titled "PanCap Adapted U.S. Government Covid-19 Response Plan" later released and marked as confidential, by the N.Y. Times. It was an outlined chart of the government's plans.
Epochtimes.com / PanCap Adapted U.S. Government Covid-19 Response Plan/ by Jeffery Tucker
https://int.nyt.com/data/documenthelper/6819-covid-19-response-plan/d367f758bec47cad361f/optimized/full.pdf

The Chart originally assigned all the rule making authority to the National Security Council (NSC) while agencies like the CDC were forced into the backseat. This information was not readily known.

Five days later FEMA became the Lead Federal Agency (LFA) as per testimony to the Senate Committee by FEMA administrator Elizabeth Zimmerman on April 14, 2021.

Why does this matter? Because Americans were misinformed by the leading state agencies for several years. It seems the State agencies have gone rogue with power and blatantly withhold truthful and pertinent information without apology.

The article went on to say, "previous pandemic plans had put HHS as the lead federal agency with the CDC carrying out the plan."

So why was this plan different? As of March 2020, the HHS, which includes the CDC, NIAID, NIH, and others had no pandemic response leadership role in implementing or determining policy.

Accordingly, our country was taken over by the National Security Agency with a large role involving the Cybersecurity and Infrastructure Security Agency. The

CISA ultimately determined who was essential and nonessential personnel.

The article went on to say there was no transparency about any of the shifting authority nor any apologies made for lying to us for years. As well as no accountability for what they did to us as a country.

Basically everything we were told, and everything reported by the 24/7 news media cycle were half-truths and lies repeated over and over again. As I'll explain in the next chapter those in control of our media use the power of the "Illusionary Truth Effect."

This is a form of brainwashing and looking back over a lifetime it has been used on Americans more and more successfully. This powerful influence of misinformation and disinformation has touched every sector of our lives. Including health, education, and cultural influences, and is often used throughout the media, music, and entertainment industries.

Meanwhile in the 2020 election cycle and all during Trump's 1st term we were inundated with dreadful news against him and about him 24/7 by the majority of the news media.

We now know those controlling the information can shut it down very easily. We have already seen this on the internet during the 2020 election cycle.

I believe Democrats wanted to continue this pandemic as long as possible. Because the mail in voting scheme was the key to their ultimate victory.

Will there be another pandemic? Another reason to shut us down, create opportunities to lie, cheat, and steal? I would not be surprised at how low the left and elite globalists will go to accomplish their goals. We have been warned; they believe in victory by any means necessary.....

The government agencies that exist to protect us continue to increase in power and authority. For example, agencies like the Food and Drug Administration.

When Robert F. Kennedy Jr. joined Trumps campaign, he said that the FDA and other agencies have been coerced and corrupted by big agriculture and big pharmaceuticals.

Some food corporations hired scientists who worked for big tobacco, in an effort to make certain unhealthy foods addictive. Why? Because there is a lot of profit to be made from sick children. If this is true, it's indefensible. https://www.youtube.com/watch?v=n15oCfLdmXI

Big Brother is Here

The FDA has approved a radiofrequency implantable chip for humans called the Veri-chip. https://www.ncbi.nlm.nih.gov/pmc/articles/PMC526112/

I wrote about this implantable chip in my first book, under the healthcare chapter, and about the consequences of socialized government healthcare.

Now that the FDA has approved an implantable chip, how long do you suppose it will be voluntary? Like so many other things, it starts off being convenient and helpful, then turns into a weapon against our freedoms and privacy.

A smaller but similar chip has been tracking your lost pets for about 15 years. Of course finding Poochie or Captain Meow was greatly appreciated. But we know it was an experimental phase in order to familiarize us with this "wonderful new tool." All who oppose it's eventual implementation will be labeled fanatics and freaks.

While I am confident it will not become mandatory until such a time as is necessary. I am still concerned of an over-reaching government, and an all-consuming healthcare system, looking to cut costs with an aging population needing increasing care.

Doctors hope that this device will improve treatment for patients in emergencies, or an unconscious person or lack of medical records. While others fear infringement on a person's personal and medical privacy.

The manufacturer of this chip is Applied Digital Systems. The chip is about the size of a grain of rice and is implanted under local anesthesia into the patients triceps area in the right arm and is invisible to the naked eye.

To activate the information a scanner is passed over the injection site and the chip displays the 16-digit number on the scanner to access the patients records securely on an encrypted internet database.

https://pubmed.ncbi.nlm.nih.gov/15528608/

Now we all know our personal information is very secure when accessed through an internet database...lol.

So the chip will be necessary for medical convenience, not for patient care, or privacy concerns. Or it's necessary for another reason, to move us toward compliance for what is yet to come. Access the link to the National Library of Medicine to read the full article for yourself.

https://www.ncbi.nlm.nih.gov/pmc/articles/PMC526112/

As Christians we should find this fascinating and exciting, witnessing prophecy coming to pass. For those who are not familiar with all this, there are no secrets kept from those who seek the truth. After all Jesus said, "Seek and you will find…"

Conditioned for Exclusivity

So I say all this because we are all being prepped for a certain future event. We see it in everyday situations.

Many years ago when Costco first opened, I was so excited to have received a one-day guest pass to shop.

I heard membership was available to union members only. I think this was to condition the population to the idea of exclusivity. Some people were allowed to shop there, while others were not.

It was before its time and apparently there were not enough members to sustain it exclusively. It did not take long to realize, at least for now, they must open it up to the public to join. But you still must buy the right to shop there; by membership only.

I was so excited to get my one-day pass by mail. I drove into New Jersey and knew exactly what I wanted to buy. I got a parking spot right in front of the store.

My kids were in school until three o'clock, so I had plenty of time; so far so good.

Shortly after I walked in the store I had a deep dread come over me. I looked around with disbelief. I actually found the item I wanted right in the front as I walked in. But I did not understand why I was so overwhelmed with a heaviness. I had planned to spend most of the day there shopping and enjoying my day pass.

I bought my item quickly and left. I started to talk aloud, like, what was that, why did I feel like that? After I calmed down I had an understanding or impression that while Costco may be a warehouse store now, I am sure one day it will become a government mandated resource distribution facility for suppling monthly rations to the people left behind and eventually only to those with the "Mark."

Well that killed the day, but as I continued to think about it, it became clear this was setting the stage for exclusivity, for members only. Do you have a card? Did you get the shot? Do you have a chip? Do you have the "Mark?"

Ready or not, it's coming. Do you feel sorry for those who choose not to join Costco? No you don't, because clearly it's their own choice.

It's only one example of setting the stage or what I call a dress rehearsal. Except at the end of days it will have life or death implications. Those who ignore the truth now will believe all the lies later. They will count their friends, family, and neighbors as enemies of the state if they don't comply or receive the "Mark." However far-fetched that may sound, it will happen.

We see now that the chip implant already exists. Many famous people, political elites, and favorite pets use it for safety purposes. It was presented as an "Angel of Light." Doctors hope it will aid in medical emergencies when a patient is unconscious; since it has been FDA approved.
https://www.ncbi.nlm.nih.gov/pmc/articles/PMC526112/

I believe both the medical implant and the ID implant will be one in the same. Complete with tracking capabilities.

Thirty years ago it was crazy to even imply this technology could be used to track or control people.

We are already in the midst of it. Times are moving quickly as electronic financial transactions have now surpassed paper transactions in December 2004. It all

sounds logical, its progressive, its more convenient, and its less time-consuming.
https://www.federalreserve.gov/boarddocs/press/other/2004/20041206/default.htm

But it's far more than that. Its intention is to control, its big brother banking. Its free now but most likely it won't be in the future. Regardless, when everything goes electronic you'll have no choice.

At some point cash will be useless and worthless. The Federal Reserve is already talking about it.

Doing away with coins first, let's see how that goes. Will people make a fuss? No we're much too comfortable.

That's why it's being done slowly. Like a pot full of lobsters, they don't know until it's too late, and they can't do anything about it.

So what does it all mean? It means information control is a commodity, those who own it also control it. Information is one of several ways Americans are being individually controlled.

As all these sectors continue to consolidate communications, media, monetary, and governmental. The more condensed power they have, the more they can control the masses.

Really what did it take for short term control of the United States during Covid? Some fear tactics, some money, and some free entertainment. Yes, we also enjoyed time with family members, some outdoor activities, and binge-watching entertainment with some free channels.

We gave up our freedoms so easily for a false sense of security. That's exactly what the unregenerate world will do after *the Rapture* and we believers are gone. Some will celebrate, but most will acquiesce very quickly in exchange for security and a sense of normalization.

Those who were skeptical to believe and were left behind, will now believe, and have to wait for persecutions and or martyrdom. Others will run for their lives for the next seven years.

My advice is to be ready for His return because the bible says it will be like a "thief in the night."

1 Thessalonians 5:2.

There were several movies that attempted to portray what this will look like. The "Left Behind" series was, I believe, the most popular.

Ready Or Not

Whether you believe what I'm about to tell you or not is irrelevant. It will happen one day. Soon many will awake to find approximately half of the world's population has disappeared. At that point it will be too late, you have entered the "Tribulation Period" on Earth.

Basically a reign of evil will take place for the next (last) seven years on Earth. Three and a half years in a false peace, and three and a half years in utter destruction as God pours out His wrath on those who rejected His love, His Son or refused to believe in Him at all.

God forbid you wake up and approximately half of the world's population has disappeared. All children under seven, maybe under ten, are gone. Planes falling from the sky because pilots have disappeared. Houses on fire because those who were cooking are gone. Car accidents because drivers have disappeared; you get the picture.

Next the world will be told a lie, maybe it was an alien abduction of half the population? They will insure it will never happen again. News organizations will be disseminating this propaganda night and day. They will proport evidence of such an event, in an effort to calm the masses. Many will choose to believe the false reports, as evidenced from past repetitions of disinformation.

How quickly will the majority comply to regain a sense of safety, security, and comfort. All who remain will be promised peace and given war. They will be promised plenty and receive scarcity.

Wars, famine, blight, unrest, and then a specific someone will rise up in the midst of all this confusion. No one will care who he is as long as he delivers some form of resolution and comfort.

All will be asked to enter into a new financial arrangement. A reset, a new world system. A system that promises provisions for all. A single mark, most likely a computer barcode such as the one we see today on every product we buy or sell.

Revelation 13:16,17

And he caused all, both small and great, rich, and poor, free and bond to receive a mark on the right hand or on the forehead.

So no one could buy or sell unless they had the mark, which is the name of the beast or the number of its name.

Once again, all those who oppose will be ostracized, cancelled, and bitterly disregarded. Abused, or worse. Eventually martyrdom is the only way out of this nightmare of your own making.

Those who receive this mark can never be saved and will be cast out of God's presence for all eternity. Not because God doesn't love you, but because you will have to deny Jesus Christ, His only beloved Son, and He is your only hope of Salvation; and you will have to pledge allegiance to this evil leader to receive his "Mark."

Those who manage to remain here without the mark after the rapture will go hungry, be homeless, friendless, running for their lives and hopeless.

For the latter three and a half years if you manage to survive, Christ will return before he strikes the earth with open seals, bowls, and plagues.

Christ will return with all who had disappeared to vanquish the enemies of God and the enemies of mankind. He will gather those who are alive and believe in Him and all who did not receive the mark. He will destroy what is left of this earth and He will create a new heaven and a new earth forever.

I share this with you because I believe the clock is ticking toward what is known as

"The Revelation of Jesus Christ."

Do not comfort yourself by thinking if you don't believe in the God of all creation you will simply just cease to exist. That's the biggest lie and one of the devil's favorite lies to tell the so-called intellectual human being.

The fact is we are all created in God's image and endowed with His attributes. He is One God Triune:

Father, Son, and Holy Spirit. We are triune having a body, soul, and (fallen) spirit. Because He is eternal, so are we. Our soul and spirit will live for all eternity in a new celestial heavenly body.

There are only two choices, either in heaven with the Lord, or apart from Him forever.

Mathew 13:50 says "Where there will be weeping and gnashing of teeth," which will first be in outer darkness, then in the *lake of fire.*

There are many bible verses that contain and confirm this phrase.

It doesn't matter if you don't believe it, or if you disagree, or you just don't care.

At the end of days there will be a "Revelation." It is truly the triumphant final battle of good over evil.

Unfortunately, the world has painted quite a frightening picture of the word "Revelation."

The word Apocalypse shares the same negative connotation. It originally meant to uncover, to disclose, and to reveal. Honestly, it means the end of this world as we know it, but reveal's God's original plan in eternity.

It will be the original plan God made for Mankind. It will disclose hidden truths that could not be erased over natural time; and finally to reveal His Only Son Jesus

Christ to the entire world, to the past, present, and future generations.

Proving that He, Jesus Christ, existed from the beginning, the Alpha and Omega, the Beginning, and the End.

Revelation: The uncovering and or "Revealing of Jesus Christ" in the heavens and on the Earth for all to see.

Ready or not He's coming. Then after that He's coming back again.... forever.

My suggestion to you is be ready the first time.

At the end of this book there will be a simple prayer, that if said with sincerity of heart, will assure you will not be left behind.

He promises that all who confess and call upon Him will be saved.

It is said if you're born twice you will only die once. If you're only born once you will die twice. Once physically, and then spiritually, when you are separated from Gods presence for all eternity.

Chapter Three

<u>Control of the Masses</u>

<u>Prince of the Power of the Air</u>

Heinrich Herz discovered and first produced radio waves in 1886.

In 1895 Italian born Guglielmo Marconi, interested in the works of Herz ,developed and marketed the first successful long-distance wireless telegraph.

In 1897 he broadcast the first transatlantic radio signal.

https://www.bbc.com/news/uk-england-somerset-61327062

In the beginning of radio broadcasting there were family radio shows, mystery shows and locals heard the news from abroad. At Christmas time families enjoyed seasonal musical favorites.

But like everything created or developed with good intentions at some point the "Prince of the power of the air" takes hold of it and perverts its original intent. Follow me for just a moment.

Originally in Heaven there was the angel named "Lucifer" meaning *light bearer*. The Bible suggests he was created with musical instruments built into his very being. He was the most beautiful of angel God had created. Lucifer led the Angelic choir in Heaven. He so desired to be like God, the Bible says, he hovered over God's throne continually.

His pride and envy culminated in his expulsion from Heaven. Since his fall, he resides between Heaven and Earth. He has many names. One of them is the "Prince of the Power of the Air."

His dark influence is behind every vile song, permissive movie, and violent video game. Now internet access allows every evil and repulsive website into your home with just a click of the mouse.

Just like Eve in the garden, he must deceive us into doing wrong, through temptations, negative messages and lies, so we will choose to do evil on our own.

With each passing year, the messages become louder, more permissive, more destructive, and more divisive than the year before. I laid this foundation so we can see his influence from a higher point of view.

Radio Media

In my opinion, the first hint of how media could affectively control the masses was experienced on October 30, 1938, it was the Mercury Theatre, on air broadcast of "The War of the Worlds." A radio version of H.G. Wells's novel, performed and broadcast live and narrated by Orson Welles. According to my research, there was no relation between the two.

The infamous radio broadcast of a Martian invasion in New Jersey was so convincing it caused a nationwide hysteria. Though unintentional, after the broadcast concluded the damage had already been done.

By the next day Mr. Welles was sure his career was over. The radio station was sued, and angry listeners threatened to shoot him on site.

www.smithsonian.com/history/infamouswar-of-the-worlds-radio-broadcast

I'm sure the passionate and powerful reaction of the public was noticed by the broadcasting hierarchy. People heard it, they believed it, and they reacted to it.

This new found power of influence was first applied in subliminal advertising. At the movies, where people did not even see the message, and they still responded favorably, and bought the products.

Media advertising has since been proven to be a very successful and powerful tool of influence over the masses.

There is no difference with medias influence over our lives today. The media company controls what we hear or recently what we don't hear. It decides what we see, or don't see, and indirectly shapes what we believe. The control is very real and very intentional.

Over the years our culture has changed, and not for the better. I will attempt to show you a slow but steady diet of counter cultural nature. From the 1950's until today, television media has completely changed the content, the culture, and the viewing of programs.

I submit to you, it was not the culture that changed the programming, but the programing that changed the culture.

Whoever owns the broadcast license chooses for us, even though we own the public airways. Although viewers complained many times along the way, the media elites accomplished a very specific purpose, still ongoing today; to fundamentally change America from within. Counter cultural programming changed our opinions, consumer appetites, and eventually our culture.

It was only a matter of time until this powerful tool would be manipulated for nefarious purposes.

Do You believe in Mind Control?

"Between 1953 and 1966 the Central Intelligence Agency financed a wide-ranging project code-named MKULTRA. Concerned with the research and development of chemical, biological, and radiological materials capable of employment in clandestine operations to control human behavior." (U.S. Supreme Court, CIAV Sims 471 US 159)

Efforts to control began in 1953 by Chemist Sidney Gottlieb, who admitted after a decade, his end goal of human mind control was impossible. Gottlieb was driven by the idea that Russia and China had already achieved these techniques and were ready to use them against our nation.

This was the creative basis for the movie The Manchurian Candidate in 1962. The movie was produced by John Frankenheimer.

https://en.wikipedia.org/wiki/Sidney_Gottlieb#Government_career

In the 1950's and in areas still mostly under American control subjects they considered expendable would be abducted or incarcerated. Then using drugs, and shock treatments conduct all manner of tests; in an attempt to wipe the brain clean and rebuild it again according to new programming.

In the end, the experiments Gottlieb conducted on his unsuspecting victims were cruel, useless, and to our knowledge, unsuccessful.

Proving only one thing, that Government officials without accountability and too much power can and will do terrible things.

Even though Gottlieb confessed after a decade that mind control is unattainable; I believe a more advanced form of mind control or mass persuasion exists and has been proven to be very effective.

The elites know this, and they use it now more than ever.

Power of The Industrial Media Complex

The success of controlling the masses, in my opinion, was realized through radio and confirmed through television. Whether by accident or coincidence, the use of its wide range of influence slowly changed our culture. Unbeknownst to us, we all have been willing participants for decades.

This strong media influence subconsciously reprograms our thinking over an extended period of time. The subtle and suggestive politically correct messages, as well as constant product advertisements reshapes what we think and what we should want.

Mass Media includes radio and television broadcasting, print media and publishing, social media communications, and the Internet. It drives our emotions, and steers our opinions, through repetitive social messaging and counter cultural suggestion. It also drives our perceived wants and needs to increase our consumer buying habits.

As Americans we were trained early on by media modes to believe everything we see is all true. And in the beginning it was, for the most part. Many adults don't believe everything they hear from news media outlets today. But a vast majority of people still prefer to get their news from television.

https://www.pewresearch.org/journalism/2018/12/03/americans-still-prefer-watching-to-reading-the-news-and-mostly-still-through-television/

To Change A Moral Nation

I submit to you that slow, subtle, and substantial changes made in television, music, and movies over a long period of time have transformed our nation. Subconsciously this was convincing us that the change was our own choice.

Moral values, family values, traditional values, patriotic values, and political values and views have all suffered a violent shift that caused a drastic change over the past 50 years.

I believe it's the reason so many people over the last few decades have been driven to divorce, suicide, violence, hopelessness, and anarchy.

Repeated negative messages can recreate the pathways in our minds. Like bad habits that are difficult to break. These thought patterns can drive us toward negative feelings of depression, anger, fear, distrust, paranoia, hopelessness, and rage.

https://maximus.com/the-brain-our-habits#:~:text=Pathways%20in%20the%20brain%20are,road%20maps%20of%20our%20brain.

Repetitive false messages and narratives are perceived as truth depending on the frequency of the message and if we believe it and accept it as truth.

If the same false messages are seen, heard, and read from similar type sources over and over, people tend to accept these as truth. Despite whether or not they are true or if they comes from an unreputable source.

This phenomenon is well established and was studied in cognitive science extensively. It's called the "Illusory Truth Effect" as documented by Lynn Hasher, David Goldstein, and Thomas Toppino in 1977. Since then many studies have reproduced the same results. (http://en.wikipedia.org/wiki/illusory_truth_effect)

Our Complicit Fake News Media

We are bombarded with faux facts, biased opinions, and false narratives every day. Which only helps to divide us and empower those who are in control of our information.

Narrative: "A representation of a particular situation or process in such a way as to reflect or conform to an overarching set of aims or values."
https://languages.oup.com/google-dictionary-en/

Our nation is divided by opposing views. If the views we have are polar opposites how can both be true? Who will be able to convince the other side their belief is the false one?

This is why we are divided not only as individuals but as a nation. Each side believing the other side is the one so egregiously misinformed.

Media networks that knowingly report false narratives or refuse to report the unbiased truth should lose their right to obtain an FCC license. Or use of the publics airways.

If they refuse to comply then pass that license opportunity to a moral creative programmer who will make something worth watching.

The influence of the news and social medias have divided this country, insisting to Americans the decline is because of the other side. I will say with certainty this message has been consistent, powerful, purposeful, and intentionally divisive, leaving us with little confidence of any long-term solutions or compromises.

We need to recognize this is a strategy of warfare.

Best said this way….

"A house divided against itself cannot stand….." Jesus said that. (Bible, Matthew12:25)

So let's awake from our sleep, understanding that if this is all purposeful then we can reverse its controlling affect. Some people believe we are already starting to do that.

Let's unfold this diabolical plan, where the few control the many as if by permission.

As previously stated there are four main types of mass media. There is print media, as in newspapers and magazines. There is broadcast media which is radio, TV, and cable television.

There is Hollywood media consisting of movies inside and outside of the home. Then there is Internet. Internet access gave birth to Social Media platforms that gave us social interaction and news cycles of information 24/7 for better or worse.

I think Social Media is proving to be the most divisive of all.

Don't take my word for it but listen to the regret expressed by some of the top engineers and creators of the social media applications we all use every day.

For example, cell phone algorithms were purposefully designed to keep you connected to your cell phone device. It keeps track of your likes, dislikes, and political preferences. So that is the information you'll receive, and it's probably ninety percent of what you will receive. It will ping you when you lay the phone down and will continue to beckon sending only "you specific" information or interests to make you reengage with the device.

Engineers created it but now they can't stop its addictive and divisive influence, its outcomes, or the consequences. I encourage everyone to watch the documentary...

"The Social Dilemma."

https://www.thesocialdilemma.com/#:~:text=From%20the%20creators%20of%20Chasing,social%20media%20and%20search%20platforms.

Fortunately, there is an awaking happening all around us. People are beginning to see that the information or misinformation we are being fed every day proves only to divide us.

Media Controlling the Masses

"I know the secret of making the average American believe anything I want him to. Just let me control television....You put something on the television, and it becomes reality. If the world outside the TV set contradicts the images, people start trying to change the world to make it like the TV set images…"

-Hal Becker, Sales Expert

Early Television

Before 1947 only a few thousand homes had a television. By 1952 half of America, approximately twelve million homes, owned a television.

The numbers continued to rise jumping to seventy-five percent of homes in 1955 and ninety-five percent of homes in 1970.

Television programming, no pun intended, began very innocently. Respect for the family, especially for the dad. Respect for traditions, and respect for the nation. Hollywood even produced religious movies we still watch today. We were united "One nation under God and indivisible."

We are anything but these days.

As stated above, by 1955 at least one TV was in seventy-five percent of American homes. Television by the mid 1950's was undergoing transition and most of the change was because television began to film, and production was moved to Los Angeles, California.

Before that eighty percent of television was broadcast live in New York. By 1960 that had dropped down to only thirty six percent. Live performances were giving way to shows being recorded on film in Hollywood tradition.

Hollywood studios like Walt Disney, and Desilu started suppling TV programming as early as 1951. By the late 1960's Sitcoms, Westerns, Soap Operas, and police and medical dramas spread across networks as television entertainment grew more popular.

There was no question that by 1960 television was the dominant mass medium in America.

The Quiz show scandal as testified to before congress in 1959 was retold in the movie Quiz Show (1994.) It was believed at the time to have tarnished television's reputation with intellectuals and civic leaders. Those who were hoping the modern technology would take the post war United States into a utopian new age.

As if driven by an unseen force; the desire of elitists and intellectuals to bring the whole world into a utopian new age will never cease. The fact is they will never stop trying. They are committed to succeed without apology.

Popular shows in the 1950's included I love Lucy, George Burns and Gracie Allen Show, Superman, Honeymooners, and Father Knows Best.

With a few exceptions, entertainment at this time was filled with action packed dramas, and comedies having little to do with contemporary issues. Why would it? It was for entertainment.

In 1959, the program "The Untouchables" aired. Robert Stack played Elliot Ness in this crime fighting drama set in the Chicago prohibition era. It had frequent displays of gun violence and police raids on criminal activities.

The show was described by many as a "cultural toxin."

Consistently portraying the worst of mankind; as anger leads to rage, and rage leads to murder. Television programming wasted no time to broadcast the worst of human nature.

Ensuring we would slowly decay from within on a steady diet of unlimited sex, crime, and violence.

Also to be taken into consideration is our fallen nature luring our senses in to watch. Our human nature is weak and drawn to the exploits of the fallen man. The seven sins if you will.

If the programming actually reflected our values as a nation why did so many people complain? Many calling for the FCC to enforce the rules of broadcasting and stop the violence and crime on television.

Parents groups, educators and other cultural watch dog groups became increasingly angry holding protests and insisting the FCC do something.

In 1961 Newton Minow joined the Kennedy Administration. He charged the FCC with ensuring the stations operated with the "public's interest" in mind.

The Federal Communications Commission is the regulatory agency that is supposed to oversee broadcasting,

Newton Minow said, "When TV is good, there's nothing better; when TV is bad, there's nothing worse." He invited the station owners to view their own stations content from sign on to sign off.

He concluded they would see a "vast wasteland" of mayhem and violence, murder, and sadism amongst other things. This speech made him famous to today.

While speaking of renewing broadcast licensing, he said " I say to you now, renewal will not be pro-forma in the future. There is nothing permanent or sacred about a broadcast license."

www.britannia.com/art/television-in-the-united-states/The-Kennedy-Nixon-debates

Newton Minow, at the time, called for more relevant programming and complained more frequently about television violence to Thomas Dodd, the head of the Senate Sub-Committee.

Mr. Minow suggested a link between television violence and crimes committed by minors and called on Dodd to investigate Juvenile Delinquency.

Subsequently the mandates given to station owners caused them to reduce violence. In 1965-1966 they produced a short season of quality programming known as "Escapist Style television."

Producer Sherwood Schwartz made a TV sit com of seven castaways on a deserted island. It was called Gilligan's Island, and was in my opinion, one of the best shows I watched. Mr. Schwartz "happened" to name the boat that stranded them on the island the S.S. Minnow.

Mr. Newton Minow passed away May 6, 2023. I applaud him for trying to hold the station owners accountable and mandating some good television for my generation to enjoy.

https://en.wikipedia.org/wiki/Newton_N._Minow

Would that more government agencies did their jobs with the same care and held their employees to the highest standards, America would be in a much better place today.

THE 1960'S and 1970's

Sherwood Schwartz went on to produce another popular program called The Brady Bunch, depicting what's known today as a blended family. Of course this family came together due to each partner losing their former spouse to death, not divorce.

In this show values were still important, and the father was still respected. There was always a moral message in the end. So It was accepted and forever in our minds as a new family nucleus.

Even though many of the shows were still doing well with young viewers, by the end of the decade, CBS decided to end those quality shows and follow NBC with more controversial shows like daytime Soap Operas and nightly entertainment such as "Rowan and Martin's Laugh In."

During this unprecedented remaking of prime-time television, within four years the entertainment industry reinvented the "Real World." The new "real world" said if it feels good do it, and or the devil made me do it. I remember those were very popular sayings.

From the 1970's we received the "real world" in regular daily doses. Displayed in every home on almost every channel….Divorce, adultery, murder, robbery, glorified crime syndicates, all common place for the next decade.

Then there was Star Trek. An outer space series of very intelligent, very amiable agnostics. Having no professed faith or belief in a deity. It's all explained away. Now God is just another life form. One of their episodes actually showed what this would look like.

No money was used, credits only. It was a colorblind society; that part was good. It showed advancing space travel on a planetary scale and working with advanced technology, some technology still being sought after or copied today. It was very before it's time.

From 1964 to 1972 there was Bewitched. Another situation comedy introducing the friendlier side of the occult. Depicting witchcraft as funny and useful, with deception, and daily drinking. I believe it also influenced the "in home" bar scene.

We too had a stand-alone modern bar set up in our living room in the late 60's to keep up with the trend. Even though neither of my parents ever drank.

It's very subtle isn't it? You can hardly see it, until you see the bigger picture in hind sight.

The sixties provided us with plenty of things to escape from. The ongoing war, the civil unrest, and an extreme feminist movement. All having their points of view, but history revealed as a nation we were beginning to unravel.

While people still complained about the sex and violence, other issues like infidelity and divorce were starting to become commonplace. Subsequently, due to no-fault divorce in the 60's the rates of divorce were rapidly increasing.

This made society less resilient to remain and fix a marriage when it was easier to cut and run. Especially if the offender, or adulterer had no more to lose than the spouse he or she betrayed.

The onslaught of attorney advertising began on June 27, 1977, from divorce to malpractice to product liability and personal injury. This opened the floodgates as attorneys encouraged all manner of personal injury lawsuits. This caused increases for everyone as auto insurances and medical liability costs rose.

Cable Breaking New Ground

In 1972 Home Box Office aka HBO was introduced
offering uncut commercial free movies and
entertainment. Over time it created original series which
were unimpressive until it joined Cinemax with
exclusive movies ladened with adult language, nudity,
and violence. HBO has since exited the erotic adult late-
night programming.

If you thought there were minimum controls over public
airwaves there is even less control over cable
programming channels. Cable has more freedoms and is
justified by its consumer base.

In the 1990's there was increasing complaints over the
amounts of violence and sex on television. It is also true
there was more religious shows and news broadcasts as
well.

Television Takes a Turn for the Worst

While shows like the Family Ties, Growing Pains and The Cosby Show still depicted functional American families, it was the peak of the culture war of television.

Simultaneously stations began introducing what was called "realistic" programming and produced shows like Married with Children, Roseanne, and The Simpsons. These were portrayed as "contemporary" American families and the new reality. Once again this probably altered the expectations for the next generation. In my opinion, these gave such a poor example of family standards and obligations.

Meanwhile crime families like The Sopranos were glorified and promiscuous lifestyles were all the rage as depicted in the popular show Sex and the City.

So America went from Father Knows Best to The Simpsons where the father knew nothing. He was portrayed as stupid and deserved no respect. The mother was the leader; the son was ignorant and inept. The older daughter was struggling with her identity. I believe the Lisa character ended up engaging in all three possible relationships from monogamy, to polyamorous, to a lesbian relationship. The problem is the show was extremely popular with most young Americans.

The negative influence and emotional damage these programs had on the perception and expectations of the next generation is probably incalculable.

This was, in my opinion, a turning point in Western Civilization's reputation.

I remember some of these shows while raising my children. It was difficult to just leave the TV on during the day. Not to mention the cartoons that were just the worst. Our saving grace was the VHS player with our favorite movies on whenever we wanted.

Though my kids did not watch most of these undermining programs in my house, they most likely watched at a friend's home. It still had a profound impact on many if not all of their generation.

Many of their friends still suffer today from a lack of confidence and identity. They are paranoid of offending everyone and still seeking group approval. Believing nothing should be judged whether it be good or evil.

You will not convince me this was unintentional.

The fact is the influence of all of the television and movies, all blatant with negative, criminal, and counter cultural messages changed America over the course of fifty years.

So many center-right families checked out and left a vast sinkhole of viewer ship unchecked, and unchallenged. This is where the counter cultural warriors wreaked havoc on our society. Through the power of the media, music, and also video games.

We went from unity to separation, married to divorced, sober minded to abusing alcohol, from law abiding citizens to increased crimes and murder.

Radical feminism to gender neutrality. Common decency to disrespect and indecency. From disagreement to division, to disassociation.

Spiraling from civil obedience to civil disobedience and eventually, if not corrected, to anarchy.

The Day the Music Died

I couldn't tell you exactly when the music began to decay. I was born in the sixties, but I remember hearing music from earlier times which spoke of heartache and divorce.

We came a long way from 100 lbs. of Clay to Lil' Jon & The East Side Boyz with Crunk Juice, boasting 784 swear words, according to an online search.

I can happily say I have never heard the song. But I'm sure many young people have.

We went from love songs to songs encouraging violence against women and law enforcement.

I miss the days when singers actually had to have talent, not just a voice. When movies did not freely take the Lord's name in vain, and comedians did not have to use expletives to be considered funny.

Facts Don't Lie

In physics, according to the second law of thermodynamics, entropy always increases with time. But the second line of its meaning suggests it's due to a lack of order; or predictability; a gradual decline into disorder.

So if we allow disorder we can expect the same results. A continued decline increasing with time from order into disorder. I believe that will apply to almost any situation.

How about lawlessness? Allowing disorder, you can expect crime to increase. So all the District Attorneys who are not prosecuting crimes large and small are feeding into the disorder and decay increasing our rapid decline toward anarchy.

Music was no exception to the rule. In the 50's and 60's you had Patti Page, Elvis Presley, and the Beach Boys, "Wouldn't it Be Nice." In the 60's we also had the Beatles "I Want to Hold Your Hand."

By the time they wrote "I am the Walrus" in the late sixties, I believe they were most likely doing psychedelic drugs…lol

In the 70's we had a short revival coupled with a nation tired of the war. Artists wrote songs reflecting these coexisting truths and emotions.

The music of the 70's was also filled with competing messages. There was a spiritual movement and Reverand Billy Graham was very popular.

In the 80's Contemporary Christian Music became very popular with hits from Rich Mullins, Amy Grant, and Stephan Curtis Chapman. It caused a temporary shift, a moral shift that I believe lasted throughout the eighties even into the 90's.

Other influences more permissive, were by Prince, Freddie Mercury of Queen, and many others contributed to Americas youth slowly being degraded.

Many artists portrayed abhorrent behavior in music videos. Some portraying people on leashes and parading around stage half naked. Unfortunately, they were idols to most teenagers at the time.

Musicians are engaging minors with this depravity while their minds are still developing. I believe producers should face charges of reckless endangerment of minors and prohibit them from making huge profits while endangering the emotional health of our youth.

The sub-genre of hip hop music called "Gangster Rap" is completely dominating an entire generation. Filling them with angst, woe, and lies, while glorifying urban street gangs and their lack of values. Depicting a world that exists primarily in the rappers mind. One he doesn't even live after the vast fortune he makes selling his music.

It feeds into a frenzy of both hate and fear and is mixed with unbridled sexuality. Objectifying young girls, who are being emotionally and physically violated in the lyrics of these popular songs. Resulting in a lack of self-respect, hopelessness, and depravity.

https://www.apa.org/monitor/julaug03/violent

The influence with music is actually increased because music speaks deep into our souls. The fallen part of our triune nature which is able to connect with our Creator. The same inner space where we connect with God through prayer, praise, and worship. These young people are being brainwashed and emotionally violated connecting with very dark messages by the lying spirits that promote all things evil.

It's not innocent, and it's not inconsequential. There are serious ramifications according to the American Psychological Association. It also should not be protected by free speech.

It should be considered endangering the welfare of a minor because it's mostly marketed and distributed to minors. https://www.apa.org/monitor/julaug03/violent

https://www.chnola.org/news-blog/2023/april/the-harmful-side-of-music-understanding-the-effe/#:~:text=However%2C%20research%20shows%20that%20music,anxiety%20or%20worsen%20existing%20conditions.

https://www.apa.org/news/press/releases/2003/05/violent-songs#:~:text=Repeated%20exposure%20to%20violent%20lyrics,only%20a%20fairly%20short%20time.

It's Only A Game

We had the same negative influences and concerns with violent video games. From Grand Theft Auto, a game about stealing cars and engaging with prostitutes. To Mortal Kombat where each round encourages you to

98

"finish him" which translates into killing your opponent. All portrayed with blood and violent images.

These were games of the 90's. Today online gaming has graduated, and the imagery has created new worlds to explore and enemies to destroy. Some displaying mythological creatures, boasting supernatural powers and magical abilities. Thousands of young adults are willingly escaping reality for fantasy.

How much is too much? No one really knows. But it is known that violent video games cause aggression, and entertainment lobbyists fought to have them all protected under free speech laws.

https://en.wikipedia.org/wiki/Brown_v._Entertainment_Merchants_Association

The First Amendment Coalition, "A group whose members include Microsoft Corp., Disney Interactive Studios Inc., Electronic Arts Inc., Sony Computer Entertainment America, and Nintendo of America, among others, also lobbied on piracy, industry ratings as well as immigration."
https://firstamendmentcoalition.org/2010/07/video-game-group-spent-1-1m-lobbying-in-2q/

Some laws were passed, and they rated the video games. The content creators still left most of the responsibilities on parents. Findings proved the ratings unhelpful, because ninety percent of the video games still portrayed violence while the content rating was approved for ten year olds. So while parents relied on ratings the kids were still exposed to unacceptable images.

https://www.health.harvard.edu/newsletter_article/violent-video-games-and-young-people.

https://www.aacap.org/AACAP/Families_and_Youth/Facts_for_Families/FFF-Guide/Children-and-Video-Games-Playing-with-Violence-091.aspx

This generation is now grown. Hopefully, many have outgrown the many addictions and daily consumption of video and online video gaming. Many have not. I believe it's why many choose to isolate, leading to depression, loneliness, and discontent. Keeping a part of their childhood experiences close feels familiar but causes them to not move forward in other arenas of life.

My hope for this next generation is to get past the lies that have damaged both men and women by distorting certain roles for generations to come.

The modification of traditional roles is inevitable. But a restructuring and denying of basic evolutionary truths which promote reproduction, and the family unit is detrimental for the survival of any modern society.

This is causing low birth rates in America and even lower marital statistics; jeopardizing the very foundations of our civil society.

I submit to you that many of these distractions perpetrated upon our youth are calculated; deceiving them with the "global warming" narrative and undermining their confidence and hope for the future. Diluting their knowledge of the truth by indoctrination,. and especially providing a false escape through fantasy worlds, and the legalization of gateway drugs in many states.

Creating the weakness and then comforting their inability to cope. Leading many to make unwise emotional decisions. All this with the intent to tether their futures into a dependence upon an ever increasing ever controlling government.

There is a major push-back. A ground swell of Center-Right Americans who are saying enough is enough. No green agenda fears, no social reconstruction. No divisive critical race theory, and no more corruption of our government agencies.

Other nations are closely watching. May we protect our future by protecting the generations to come.

God help us, God forgive us, God deliver us from the evil time. God bless America.

In the Palm of Your Hands

The social media addiction of our nation is unprecedented. Not only do we have access to a 24/7 news and information, we can't even guarantee the information we are receiving is the truth.

In this chapter I spoke about the ability of the "Industrial Media Complex" to influence our opinions and drive our decisions.

All the repetition of negativity and error is making our brain paths unable to discern truth from lies. This is intentionally used today, in my opinion, by the many fake news outlets, pushing the corrupted political ideology and agendas of the left.

They accuse the "right" of these same tactics. Americans are being tossed back and forth with competing truths. I think it's making all of us skeptical causing a deep distrust of opposing views.

Even the seasoned print medias are slanted left and often corrected or forced into a retraction. This happens after the damage has already been done. So we don't really know if what we hear or read is the basic truth.

Now with Artificial Intelligence it will be almost impossible to know if what we are seeing is true. This is so dangerous because it affects everything. Something fake can appear real. Something real can be said to be fake. Mass confusion is on the horizon if America does not control the unleashing of the power of A.I.

It was said by a guest speaker at a church that the sin which caused the fall of Mankind was not the act of Eve eating the apple. It was Eve wanting the knowledge of good and evil separate and apart from God. Without His permission or protections. In essence it was the idea of her becoming like (a) God.

Eve was deceived but it's said Adam took freely from his wife. So he was held responsible according to the scriptures. I agree and believe that this was the temptation that caused them to fall in the Garden of Eden.

God warned them both that to consume this knowledge apart from Him would surely bring forth death and it did. Physical and spiritual death came into the world, along with every other vile thing like sin, sickness, pain, and all manner of evil.

The Speaker proceeded to say that today this generation without a conscience toward God holds the knowledge of good and evil in the palms of their hands every day.

This knowledge includes our smart phones and computer devices that enable us to access vast amounts of information instantaneously for the asking at the touch of a button.

Some would say "the knowledge is used for good, it's all good.." Free speech, free press…

Knowing full well many have already died from the unbridled access of information and communications online. More often than not mankind tends towards the reprehensible on the Internet.

In this Chapter I also stated A.I. may be or can be connected to the future unholy trinity of the Anti-Christ. After some time thinking about it I am fully convinced it will be.

Because in the end times, the Anti-Christ will not work alone. He will have what's known as an unholy trinity. Consisting of himself, the beast, and the false prophet; a religious type figure head.

I believe A.I. is or will be considered "the beast." A culmination of all human knowledge and history, both good and evil. Created with algorithms, which will make it appear as a problem solving entity.

It will be considered flawless made up of mankind's collective intelligence. It's being built upon now and many are knowingly and unknowingly contributing to this vast network.

It may still take time but once completed it will rival any source of human intelligence. It will have all the knowledge and answers that man desires to have… separate and apart from God.

Hey Alexa, Why Am I ?

This last generation in America has grown up fairly prosperous without the need to dig deep or pray hard. Many don't even know about what Jesus has done for them on the Cross. Many don't care to know.

When we want information we pick up our "palm god" and get the answer we need very quickly. Or we call out to a domestic standing unit waiting, and listening by the way, for our next request.

We have ostensibly removed God from our culture. While He remains still, we do not acknowledge or honor Him as a nation as we did in past generations.

There are Godless groups that exist in America with the sole purpose of erasing God from this country. One day soon it will happen.

As we continue to tear each other apart we are eroding the trust anyone can have in human nature. We are ushering in a revolution of cybernetic social hierarchy. https://interactions.acm.org>view

Most people won't need any convincing at all. Artificial Intelligence is the perfect answer for the "let me live my life, make my own decisions, make this easier, I'm okay on my own," society.

It's impartial, its logical, pervasive, and gets the job done without emotion or regret. It will seemingly help me make the best decisions for *Me*. It will be very easy for this next generation to entrust more and more of life's decisions to a non-human entity without bias. Or at least that's how it will appear.

This new technology is far more sinister than it seems. It's a preset strategy that will encompass the globe. Many are trying to usher it in. You may have heard of the Global Reset, or the New World Order.

But know this, your comfort and your desires will not be considered important after all.

The complete takeover of global-nomics, with the help of AI, will not be seen until it's too late. Then many will awaken, many will not care, and many will already be gone.

Chapter Four

"The problem with Socialism is that eventually you run out of other people's money."

British Prime Minister Margaret Thatcher

Globalization V Sovereignty

The Global Push in America

In America, the push for globalization started with NAFTA under the Clinton administration but reached its pinnacle under President Obama. By passing the Affordable Care Act in March of 2010 we essentially started government controlled healthcare in America, which is the first step toward Socialism.

In my opinion, Obama was not raised to be and is not pro-American. Was it due to the Marxist influencers in his life? Maybe his socialist mother and or his socialist grandfather? Was it because of Anti-Colonialism sentiment, which has been pushed on college campuses for decades. Is it because he is biracial? I don't know, and personally I really don't care.

Barack and Michelle were not under-privileged in their youth as minorities. Nor were they automatically entitled to anything. Barack Obama's maternal grandmother was a bank president, and Michelles father was a civil servant, as was mine.

I suspect the young Obamas may have received extra considerations on their college entrance applications and scholarships due to affirmative action.

They rose to the heights of political power very quickly. He ascended from a community organizer to President after serving less than two years in the US Senate.

During their terms, I believe they intentionally separated Americans across every possible dividing line. A topic I wrote about in my first book.

I believe he was a socialist, and not because he "shared his toys." Now he appears to be more of an elite globalist. This allows him to be considered an intellectual while remaining unapologetically wealthy.

He ran his campaign on "change." But nothing changed for the people on the South Side of Chicago. Nothing changed but Obama's address, from the State House to the White House.

Many of today's globalists and green purveyors are wealthy. Take for instance John Kerry and Al Gore.

They both believe Americans must have less and do less in order to save the planet, while they keep their private jets and mega homes.

Hypocrites to say the least.

https://www.bostonherald.com/2022/07/14/whitbeck-john-kerrys-stonewalling-strategy-is-running-out-of-gas/

https://www.investors.com/politics/editorials/al-gores-climate-change-hypocrisy-is-as-big-as-his-energy-sucking-mansion/

There are many people who fall under this delusion. Having obtained much wealth, they believe they have earned the right to pick and choose who has, and who has too much, and now must share.

But the rules never apply to them.

Let's be clear, it's not because elites actually care about people. It's because they want the accolades for trying. It makes them feel better about themselves and look better in the eyes of others.

But the global elites can't begin to save the whole world without all of the money, your money. Collectively the wealthy elitists have most of the money. They want to keep their money, power, and lifestyle, while at the same time control the rest of us to finance their green global vision of utopia.

Globalization: The United Nations agenda for global redistribution of wealth.

In my first book I said that globalization is "not necessarily good for America." While I'm not against fair trade between the nations, I am against shipping American jobs and tax monies overseas.

I am also against any consolidation of powers, where the few try to control the many.

America has earned the right to be a leading nation. We sacrificed our blood, time, not to mention our financial support to set nations free.

America is the largest assessed Nation-State in the world and is the largest voluntary contributor to the United Nations. Yet the U.N. favors many nations who contribute far less and are hostile to America and our allies, namely Israel.

In my opinion it's a world council that corrupts everything it touches and continually depletes the finances of the western nations.

In return for our contributions, it votes against the U.S. and Israel consistently. We are ignorant to continue to support such an inept organization that bids for our demise at every meeting.

Monies sent and spent to help the poor and needy should be reallocated to organizations that succeed without corruption. I can name several.

Under President Biden, I'm sure U.N. support was increased again since 2021. Especially under the democratic congress, I don't even have to fact check it.

USAID has also received an increase in budget. This is more money fleeced from the American taxpayers and given to the less fortunate but only after being funneled through the pockets of some of the most corrupt leaders and bureaucrats that exist on planet Earth.

https://nypost.com/2015/10/11/the-long-sordid-tale-of-corruption-un-leadership/

https://www.economist.com/unknown/2005/08/09/corruption-at-the-heart-of-the-united-nations

Some leaders of smaller nations that receive large contributions from the US, and through the U.N. don't want their people to succeed.

Some corrupt leaders thrive when their people are solely dependent on them. By purposely keeping them poor we are pressured to continue to increase our annual financial aid. It also allows them to control their people with the mere promise of food and water.

Our tax dollars continue to line the pockets of many corrupt foreign leaders and very little gets to the people who need it most.

The Nobel Prize Economist Milton Friedman once said,

"One of the great mistakes is to judge policies and programs by their intentions rather than their results."

This posted on a website from Global Issues reads…..

> "A former UN Secretary-General, the outspoken Kofi Annan of Ghana, once said that "billions of dollars of public funds continue to be stashed away by some African leaders even while roads are crumbling, health systems are failing, and school children have neither books nor desks nor teachers, and phones do not work."
> https://www.globalissues.org/news/2021/06/07/2 8013

Except today many of the same corrupt leaders are now keeping the money and sending their people directly to America. Approximately 10 million people from 126 nations have illegally crossed our southern border since

Biden and Harris took office. So Americans can continue to pay again, and again.

We are amazingly stupid, and this is one of many reasons why we find ourselves still battling the war on drugs, poverty, and hunger today.

The United Nations was established in October 1945 after WWII. It was the best hope for maintaining world peace through cooperation.

In recent years I believe it's done more harm than good and it's time has come to an end. I believe it has spawned immense worldwide corruption like a cancer that has metastasized without cure.

Our leaders are well aware of this and are equally culpable. It is unsustainable and needs to be defunded.

A Tale of Two Ideologies

Very simply put there are two opposing forces fighting for the soul of America.

One is freedom, self-reliance coupled with a sincere brotherly love. A Judeo Christian perspective was the founding principle America was built upon.

Freedom; freedom of religion, of speech, and of truth in the free press. All of these ideas are under severe attack and barely exist anymore in America.

For the first time in America's history our founding principles and freedoms may not survive.

This country was built on the tenants of life, liberty, and the pursuit of happiness. Those truths still stand in the hearts and minds of true Americans.

In America everyone can become anything they want if they are willing to work for it and compete by the same rules as everyone else.

We are to pursue our talents and passions to the benefit of all mankind. It is said,… "rising tides lift all ships."

We do not exist to be subjects to the benefit of a bloated government, so they can tax and spend us into deficits that cannot be repaid.

No Life for Julia

The other idea or ideology is the "nanny state" mindset. Where the government provides all your needs from cradle to grave. This is not the American dream. Obama tried to sell this idea hoping he could persuade young Americans to settle for less, and it was pathetic. https://www.cnn.com/2012/05/09/opinion/bennett-obama-campaign/index.html

Let's be clear. Socialists, Marxists, and Globalists are all the same, egalitarians with one purpose; redistributing America's wealth here at home and around the world.

Making the US of no consequence, without influence, without wealth, and without power. All people equally poor, except for the elite architects of the scheme.

Why? In order to exert their vision of a One World Utopia. Using the global warming, climate change mantra as its religion to unite the masses.

While at the same time keeping the third world countries under developed and financially dependent upon UN state nation contributions. So they can never fully develop or be independence from the support of wealthier nations.

I believe this is how they intend to contain global warming. To not allow underdeveloped nations the opportunity to develop and cause more pollution. If you read between the lines of the U.N. charters for economic development you will see this is true.

It's a global economic scheme with the wealthiest players gaining the most in position, power, and profits. All the rest of us in America and all of the Western European nations will just get to pay for it.

Poorer nations will supposedly benefit by engaging in lifelong learning, barely escaping their subpar living conditions, due to global warming restrictions and U.N. mandates

https://www.greenclimate.fund/gcf-2#:~:text=The%20Green%20Climate%20Fund's%20second,over%20the%20next%20four%20years.

https://www.greenclimate.fund/document/strategic-plan-green-climate-fund-2024-2027

Except all the money in the world won't create their version of heaven on earth, but that won't stop them from trying.

If they are not stopped, it is going to get much worse for everyone. Much worse than we can imagine.

They are a godless society playing God with the world's finances and resources. The spirit that drives them is unholy, dishonest, subversive, and all consuming. It consolidates power to a few and robs the many of their goods, freedoms, as well as their God given potentials.

Where's the Beef

If this global warming madness is allowed to continue I'm sure it will plunge many into poverty and eventually cause global food shortages.

The One Party Global legislature will insist that the global warming crisis needs to be addressed immediately. They will push for global or U.N. legislation for suppliers of meat and dairy farmers to kill off cattle to save the earth from additional global warming.

This is being debated now. Those in charge of climate change and the green agenda are truly pushing this madness.

Culling: is selective slaughter, for reducing animal populations.

https://www.europarl.europa.eu/doceo/document/E-9-2023-002312_EN.html

https://www.foxnews.com/media/peta-calls-climate-change-plan-culls-200000-cows-ridiculous-government-kill-squads-wont-help

https://thebulletin.org/2023/10/ireland-isnt-culling-cows-for-climate-but-maybe-they-should-be/#:~:text=The%20Food%20Vision%20Dairy%20Group,additives%20a

Unfortunately, when the famines come, the third world nations will be the first to go before all the wealthy who are in control.

When that fails to be enough, they will start eliminating non-compliant political opponents.

It's not too hard to believe because there will be more hunger, less food, and more opposition.

We are beginning to see states like New York suing for proposed unrealistic green gas reduction quotas.

These lawsuits cannot be achieved without dismantling many successful companies and destroying many jobs. This will also increase food prices for everyone. Rest assured more lawsuits will come unless we unseat all of the rogue and lawless representatives.

https://nypost.com/2024/03/04/opinion/tish-james-is-turning-new-york-into-a-banana-republic-with-yet-another-lefty-lawsuit/

Most of our problems have simple solutions.

Take meat production. I agree that all cattle should be treated with kindness, given green grass to feed on, and be able to live as free as possible.

The mass food production is not healthy for the animal or for the human who consumes it. It's also down right cruel. The solution is to allow more farmers to cultivate more of the land. Allowing the cows and other farm animals to fertilize the land naturally. Then the meat will be healthier and in more abundance. The soil will also regenerate and produce the missing minerals we all need.

The outcome may be a little more expensive at first, but if farmers can make some money they will begin to participate.

The problem is that mass production facilities don't allow smaller farmers to compete. Mass production of anything drives the price lower. But the answer is not eliminating beef productions or it's consumption altogether.

Let producers buy or lease entire areas if they can produce the product without high methane production, in a humane and reasonable fashion.

Give cattle farmers open untaxed land to raise grass fed beef, to help reduce the problem. It should be given to American farmers before it is sold to foreign entities like China through third party buyers. Which, by the way, should be illegal in every state.

The American consumer is already changing their beef preferences, which drives the free market demand in the right direction. This is only one of many examples.

Americans succeed best when left alone to make their own decisions free from excessive government controls.

Undermining America's Stability:

Step One to undermining America is to eliminate the American dream, question American ideals, and separate the American family. Reorder it, change it, bankrupt it, to divide and conquer.

Meanwhile socialists and globalists continue to persuade the unchallenged masses that they cannot succeed on their own. They are told or perceive that they have less because others have more.

Unfortunately, ignorant people of all races believe this lie, and those are the masses which drive the Socialist movement in America. Couple this with millions of illegals who come from poorer socialist nations, and we have a real problem in America.

Today Americans who have some type of success are being over taxed and or over regulated to give up what they have worked hard for in the name of fairness and equity.

Blurring the lines of Equality

Equity and equality are not the same thing. Equality is equal opportunity in everything. That is everyone being given the same opportunity to apply and succeed.

While this was not the case many years ago, times have changed, and it is the case today.

Equity is attempting an equal distribution amongst everyone whether they earned it or not. That's how most people see it, and that's why it does not work.

It causes more division, resent, and contempt between the races. Which is supposedly opposite of the desired effect. But the pendulum has swung to the opposite extreme causing discrimination once again.

Diversity hiring is nothing new, the idea is a kin to affirmative action. Since the death of George Floyd, many companies have pushed harder for Diversity, Equity, and Inclusion training and hiring practices.

Many hospitals, and other large corporations like Amazon, Boeing, Google, and Alphabet, to name a few have been using forced hiring practices based on diversity, equity, and inclusion. Today it is simply known as DEI hiring preferences.

https://www.resourcefulfinancepro.com/news/dei-hiring-gone-awry/

This is clearly discrimination if an applicant is not as qualified for the position but fits only the desired demographic. To be clear, any color but white. Qualified applicants should be chosen based on their qualifications and experience, not their color, and most people agree with this sentiment.

https://www.resourcefulfinancepro.com/news/dei-hiring-gone-awry/

Affirmative action caused reverse discrimination according to the equal protection clause under the 14th Amendment. Affirmative Action was overturned by the Supreme Court on June 29, 2023.

As a nation we implemented the original Civil Rights Act in 1866, followed by the 14th Amendment granting equal protection under the law and citizenship to all previously under slavery or transported here for that purpose.

https://www.senate.gov/artandhistory/history/civil_rights/background.htm#:~:text=The%20Thirteenth%20Amendment%2C%20ratified%20by,including%20the%20right%

The Civil Rights Act was amended in 1965 then passed again. It was passed despite the Democrats who waged a political war and warned against it. It passed with the help of the Republicans.

President L.B. Johnson signed it into law without Democrat support. This version included a provision to outlaw public segregation.

https://www.archives.gov/milestone-documents/civil-rights-act#:~:text=Despite%20Kennedy's%20assassination%20in%20November,theaters%2C%20restaurants%2C%2

Immediately the Democrat party proposed the Welfare programs that were detrimental to minority families. I believe it was to undermine their ability to truly benefit from the civil rights victory they received. These programs promised financial help, but only under circumstances that guaranteed minorities would remain financially dependent for generations. This was political revenge, and it would keep minorities on the " Democrat plantation" as loyal voters for decades to come.

https://www.aei.org/articles/seduced-how-radical-ideas-on-welfare-work-and-family-sent-poor-black-americans-to-hell/

Socialist Democrats pretend to promote minorities by lowering standards and making it easier. Because they really believe minorities can't compete any another way.

Thus they pretend to be advocates, but in reality they deny them the success of reaching their full potential.

When everyone competes by the same rules of performance and qualifications, everyone is celebrated for their success. That is the essence of the American dream, and equal opportunity.

I think Elon Musk said it best as reported by the Washington Post…..

"Diversity, Equity and Inclusion" are propaganda words for racism, sexism, and other "-isms."

This is just as morally wrong as any other racism and sexism. Changing the target class doesn't make it right!"

— Elon Musk (@elonmusk) December 16, 2023

Since the Supreme Court ruling on affirmative action in June 2023, many corporations are now pushing back on DEI policies. Many due to budget cuts, not because of the policy per say.

I submit to you that some corporations are under scrutiny due to under-qualified people receiving special treatment because of DEI. Lawsuits are rising and corporations are now taking the off ramp.

Affirmative action, and now DEI were supposed to erase the perceived imbalance?

All it did was undermine the legitimacy of true success for many successful minority students and professionals.

This should never be.

This was caused by lowering the qualifying scores for colleges and medical schools. Women were given less weight and distance qualifications to be a fire(wo)man. Affirmative action was supposed to help achieve an equal outcome, not equal opportunity.

In conclusion, someone's color or gender should not qualify or justify someone's promotion or professional success.

I can think of several examples of *Firsts* that have completely disappointed.

1) President Barack Hussain Obama became the first African American President at a time when America had nearly forgotten about racial division.
   He quickly reminded us of our past mistakes, again, and again. Regurgitating the same old hate and perceived inequities in order to win the White House. Some voted out of new hope; others out of white guilt with hopes the charge of racism would finally disappear from America. Not a chance, it was just the beginning of the plan. In my opinion he set us back forty years in race relations and national unity.

2) Kamala Harris the first black, first female Vice President. I watched her in the Democratic Primary, accusing VP Joe Biden of being a racist during the debates. Maybe somehow to prove her wrong or by the higher powers that be, Biden chose her as his running mate. Quite astonishing.

She received less than two percent in that primary amongst the other Democrats running. In my opinion she was chosen because of diversity issues.

She became the Democrat nominee for President in 2024 without one person in any state primary casting a vote for her. It was said Nancy Pelosi and Barack Obama caused then President Biden to step down from the race. Then Biden put his delegated votes behind Kamala.

During the primary season, the Democrats blocked, sued, and stopped RFK Jr. and Marianne Williamson from even posing a challenge to President Biden. So much for Democracy.

It took the Obamas several weeks to publicly endorse then VP Kamala Harris.

https://www.facebook.com/SkyNewsAustralia/videos/barack-obama-wants-open-contest-after-refusing-to-endorse-kamala-harris/2184339878613932/

3) Attorney General (D) Latisha James of New York: The first African American and first woman to hold this position. She promised during her AG campaign to prosecute a political

opponent. Thus conducting lawfare against then former President Trump, trying to remove his assets and his businesses in New York City. Unprofessional and legally unconscionable.

She accused former President Trump of fraud by over estimating the values of his properties. There are many, but particularly his Florida homestead at Mar-a-Lago. The problem with her case was the state concluded his real estate values based on opinion, not actual real estate values.

She said he committed fraud by over valuing these properties to the bank for loans. The loans Donald Trump obtained were scrutinized by each bank that loaned him money. All the loans were repaid. The banks testified on Trump's behalf and said they would gladly loan him money again. There were no victims here. Yet she claim fraud without a victim of fraud.

It's election interference since he was the presumptive candidate for the 2024 Republican party. We know this because of the many indictments against the former President, in my opinion they were all coordinated by the current Biden/Harris Department of Justice.

https://reason.com/volokh/2024/01/14/new-yorks-civil-lawsuit-against-trump-is-unconstitutional/

I also believe AG James violated Donald Trump's civil rights and should be held accountable.

She ran her campaign on prosecuting Trump and she literally said, " He's too male, too pale, and too stale…."

Very prejudicial statements if you ask me. Also not reasons to target someone for prosecution. It's sexist, blatantly racist, and it's discrimination against his age.

https://politicsny.com/2018/05/09/james-male-pale-stale-comments-could-affect-her-ag-plans/

There are other "Firsts" that were extremely disappointing. Just because it's a first for something, does not mean it's the best for America.

A Forced Decline

Let's return for a moment to 2009. It was said Obama was a law professor at Harvard. He was not a law professor. He was an adjunct professor, a part time college instructor, a lecturer, hired by contract.

Obama lectured on the book Rules for Radicals by Saul Alinsky. The methods of community organizing. It's how to overwhelm the system in order to "change" it by applying the principals of the egalitarians redistribution of wealth. In other words Socialism.

We are seeing the forced decline of our nation being accelerated before our eyes.

Globalists persuade the simple or underachieving, "We should all be financially equal, we should all have the same; regardless of experience, participation, or personal achievements.

Poorer nations are now responding by allowing swarms of illegal and criminal illegal immigrants to violate the southern border connected to America, and other Western European nations without restrictions. Coming by flights, boats, railway caravans, and on foot.

South American nations, namely Venezuela, are reportedly emptying their jails, while others are encouraging their young male populations to retreat from their own countries and make the trek to America. All while these same countries continue to receive financial aid from America.
https://www.thecentersquare.com/texas/article_4e58d58 6-3db2-11ed-a3dd-43b7f5bf6866.html

One spokesperson on YouTube, Victor Davis Hansen of the Hudson Institute, suggested these South American countries are allowing their young men to leave "to avoid revolution in their own countries due to a lack of jobs, provision, and opportunity."

So why are we and other Western Europeans being forced to absorb and support the worlds woes.

The decline of America and Europe is seen as necessary by top global leaders in order to provide the basics for the world. They believed the wealthier nations should and now must have their wealth redistributed.

It is necessary to reduce America's influence, financial position, and our sovereignty. It's also an attempt to change America's long-term demographic. To take America down a peg. As Barack Obama promised "to fundamentally change America."

Joe Biden and Kamala Harris are implementing the same destructive policies that Barack Obama started. Many of the same people who worked for Obama were held over in the State Department, and other government agencies. I also believe this is serving as Obama's third term, vicariously accomplishing through Biden/Harris what he could not accomplish in his first two terms.

Unconstitutional immigration reform. Knowing that national sovereignty must be erased to attain true globalization.

That's why we see this massive unregulated violation of many sovereign borders both here and abroad.

God Established the Nations : ...and the boundaries of their dwellings….. Acts 17: 26-27.

America has always stepped in to help other nations during times of natural disaster and human suffering.

But since the 1940's our government leaders have intervened and destabilized various Nation-States around the world.

We used the power of the "military industrial complex," and money that was once considered charitable, to buy, sell, install, and protect dictators around the world.

By doing this we caused great corruption and are now reaping the consequences for many years of unnecessary and uncharitable interventions.

https://en.wikipedia.org/wiki/United_States_involvement_in_regime_change

Under the U.N. Refugee Agency there are listings of government and non-governmental agencies working together, not for the occasional refugee crisis, no, I believe they were implementing and causing all the immigration crises around the world.

There were ten national and state partners, which included Dept. Homeland Security and Health Human Services, under the Biden and Harris Administration.

There were three non-government resettlement agencies, and ten international organizations for migration.

In my opinion, all working together to expedite a worldwide outcome of forced immigration.

Despite the fact that this forced US immigration was against US immigration laws, and the desire of American people.

Enemies Both Foreign and Domestic

Alejandro Mayorkas- Deputy Director of Homeland Security was born in Havana, Cuba. His family fled during the Cuban revolution. He grew up in Beverley Hills, California and attended U.C Berkeley.

https://en.wikipedia.org/wiki/Alejandro_Mayorkas

He was appointed by President Clinton, promoted by President Barack Obama. Under Biden he led the Department of Homeland Security and was impeached for dereliction of duty, after hearings were held by the 118th U.S. House of Representatives.
https://www.texastribune.org/2024/01/10/texas-republicans-mayorkas-impeachment/

He was not removed from his position because then Senate Majority Leader (D) Chuck Schumer would not bring the Articles of Impeachment to the Senate floor for a vote.

This has never happened before in the history of the US Senate. Some Congressional Representatives, and some of foreign birth are leading the way to undermine Americas future.

All American voters should take notice <u>and vote out the Democrats who actively support Socialism and +terrorist groups</u> that wish to harm America, and our ally Israel.

All self-proclaimed Socialists, including (D) Senator Bernie Sanders of Vermont, should be expelled from Congress and barred from reelection. You cannot represent agendas diametrically opposed to the US Constitution, individual independence, and American values and still be fit for high public office in America.

<u>Where do your loyalties lie?</u>

We are being undermined internally on a governmental level, and externally by so-called American citizens, who are organizing, funding, and supporting caravans from other countries worldwide to invade our southern border.

The migration of these millions of illegal immigrants is supported by many different nonprofit organizations like Catholic Charities. As well as globalists hell bent on wide open borders.

Millions have come over unhindered, and are supplied with cell phones, food, clothing, and debit cards.

Housing, food, and healthcare are funded by taxpayer dollars once they arrive.

https://www.heritage.org/homeland-security/heritage-explains/who-helping-biden-facilitate-americas-border-crisis

In the past we have had many illegals come across the border. In the 1980's President Ronald Reagan granted amnesty to millions of illegals and promised it would never happen again.

I believe they were primarily from Mexico, and for the most part they assimilated into society. I don't remember hearing about migrant crime. It seemed they were happy to be here, expected to work, and had a grateful attitude while becoming American citizens.

Today many crimes are committed by illegals. As I said earlier some southern border nations are emptying their jails and sending criminals north to America. https://www.thecentersquare.com/texas/article_4e58d58 6-3db2-11ed-a3dd-43b7f5bf6866.html

The current immigration crisis is unprecedented and has broken every record to date and each year's numbers increase over the previous year.

Many of these people no longer respect America. They may want our freedoms and opportunities, but I believe their loyalties lie elsewhere and may never be loyal to America.

Some are actively using our legal system against Americans who criticize or object to their being here, and or their receiving of public tax dollars.

We must also address foreign nationals who have over-stayed a visa, as well as any student with a visa actively participating in riots or recruiting for anti-American organizations or on social media. These people should be deported immediately and not be allowed to reenter America again for any reason.

End Game First scenario /Election Interference by Numbers

Why would Biden and Harris allow this crisis to continue?

As the illegal immigrants continue to flow into the country some blue states like New York are providing financial assistance. Minnesota is allowing illegal immigrants to apply for driver's licenses.

https://www.dailysignal.com/2024/08/06/kamala-harris-vp-pick-signed-bill-allowing-illegal-aliens-receive-drivers-licenses-minnesota/#:~:text=In%20March%202023%2C%20Minnesota%20Gov,licenses%20regardless%20of%20immigration%20status.

When applying for a driver's license, the DMV asks if you want to register to vote. This is no joke.

Democrats wish to be paid back with Democratic votes. If not now than in the near future as they push for a pathway to citizenship for all illegal immigrants. They wish to tip the scale blue forever.

https://nypost.com/2024/07/28/us-news/elizabeth-warren-says-11m-illegal-migrants-need-pathway-to-citizenship-suggests-kamala-harris-will-work-to-get-it-done/

Blue states are bleeding people. Many people are leaving blue states because they are over taxed and are considered higher crime areas.

So blue states need more people, many people, they need their numbers to be higher. This administration is trying to get as many illegals processed as possible.

This serves Democrats well by increasing the census population in blue states they can receive more funds from the federal government.

It also allows them to have more congressional seats allotted in Democratic areas. While at the same time reducing the size of what would be Republican majorities.

States like New York have already proposed to let illegals vote in the local elections. Republicans had to sue the city council, and on appeal won the case that struck down the local law.

https://nypost.com/2024/02/21/us-news/nyc-non-citizen-voting-law-struck-down-as-unconstitutional/

https://council.nyc.gov/joseph-borelli/2024/02/23/nycs-non-citizen-voting-law-ruled-unconstitutional-on-appeal/

The continuation of blatant acts of unconstitutional laws attempting to be pushed through without notice is Un-American. California already allows non-citizens to vote in some local elections.

https://www.latimes.com/california/story/2024-07-19/federal-law-bans-noncitizens-from-voting-for-president-but-not-in-these-local-california-elections

Illegal immigrants should never have the right to vote in any American elections.

End Game Second Scenario / Election Interference…*by Any Means Necessary*

So the continued baseless indictments against Former President Trump is only proving to most Americans that the Dept of Justice, some State Department officials, and the Biden /Harris White House are all compromised.

They are working together to try to keep Trump from being in the 2024 election.

America, this is truly election interference at its finest.

Now if they can't keep him from running, then they'll try to keep him from winning by ruining his reputation. What if that doesn't work?

Since the 2020 election there has been an overhaul of some state voter rolls by conservative organizations, and some Republican state assemblies to "clean house."

Republicans also pursued the swing states that changed voting laws without the input of their state legislative assemblies. That was not lawful.

https://www.texasattorneygeneral.gov/news/releases/ag-paxton-sues-battleground-states-unconstitutional-changes-2020-election-laws

So there have been some changes for the good with regard to updated voting rules.

Some voter rolls have been purged, and some states have implemented voter ID laws as well.

Democrats always accuse Republicans of being racist because we want voter ID. Identification to vote should be mandatory in every state of the union and would increase the confidence we have in our election process.

The Counting Process

Red states like Texas and Florida have rejected some of the counting machines and thank God that Democrats were not able to turn Texas or Florida blue.

https://thetexan.news/elections/2020/texas-rejected-use-of-dominion-voting-system-software-due-to-efficiency-issues/article_480803c0-a7af-5b2f-bc21-e29661d5bd07.html

Now even some conservative counties in California are ending their contracts early with some voting machine companies.

https://www.cnn.com/2023/04/11/politics/dominion-fox-news-voting-machines/index.html

I believe the same people who swore Trump didn't win in 2016 perfected the system (which they accused Russia of interference) and won in 2020. If you don't believe it can happen watch "Kill Chain" Cyber War on America's elections.

They certainly proved that "everything is hackable," and these machines are still being used in 28 states.

A Wikipedia post stated….

"The film examines the American election system and its vulnerabilities to foreign cyberwarfare operations and 2016 presidential election interference." The film also features hackers at the conference DEF CON in their attempts to test the security of electronic voting machines."

https://en.wikipedia.org/wiki/Kill_Chain:_The_Cyber_War_on_America%27s_Elections

https://www.imdb.com/title/tt12041084/reviews

In 2016 many were trying to say Trump did not win the election. In this film, which was slanted left, I believe Democrats employed these tactics in 2020. Knowing full well how it can work to steal the 2020 election.

Nevertheless, the Supreme Court did nothing about it because the red states certified the fraudulent votes and sealed the election for Biden.

Once that happened, SCOTUS could not touch a legally certified election. Trump was confident that VP Pence could help but it was too late.

Protesting for Me but not for Thee

Americans were so distraught knowing in the depths of their souls that the election was stolen. They gathered on January 6th to exercise their right of free speech, and to peacefully protest.

The opposition was well aware of the passion of the wronged crowds. So, democrat leaders dispatched enemies into the Conservative camp. Spies made up of many opposing groups and were dressed to look like MAGA Republicans.

Government FBI agents and assets were among the crowd as well.

Pelosi did not call for the National Guard. The media blocked the fact that Trump offered the National Guard, and she refused. Yet a web search, even today, will give you many fake posts and fake news reports from practically every news source. It should scare you the way the deep state controls, twists, and blatantly lies to the America people, through the liberal media outlets.

https://www.gop.gov/news/documentsingle.aspx?DocumentID=102

I believe Pelosi was made aware of the intel and formed a contingency plan. Since all these people showed up, they would use it to take attention off of the stolen election. They called it an "Insurrection" and this is all we heard from the media for the next three and a half years.

We are Conservatives, we don't destroy public property and hurt innocent people. We don't dress in tactical gear and wear military face masks, scale buildings and cause violence.

If you removed the news media vocal commentary and just watched the people quietly walking through the

Capital, nothing was disruptive, or violent. I was watching on Cable news.

I saw the Capital police waving the people into the building and pointing which way to go.

Yes, there were a few troublemakers. Some think they were infiltrators, and I tend to agree. They caused minor damage comparatively to other protests.

No police officers were killed on January 6th. Even though you heard it repeated many times. Once again it's not true.

https://www.nationalreview.com/2022/03/no-cops-died-in-the-line-of-duty-during-the-capitol-riot/

https://www.foxnews.com/opinion/tucker-carlson-reason-leaders-hid-january-6-tapes

Unfortunately one patriot died. Her name was Ashli Babbit. She was killed by then Capitol Hill Police Officer Michael Byrd. He said he discharged his weapon after his verbal order was not followed.

No one physically resisted him, no one had weapons drawn. I think he panicked, and now she's gone.

Ashli Babbit was a U.S. Airforce patriot who served our nation for twelve years.

It was said that she was trying to stop others from breaking into the door. I believe that to be true. She was married to Aaron Babbit, who was thirty-nine at the time and she did not have any children.

January 6th was amplified in order to chill the free speech of the Conservative opposition. It was all media hype combined with misinformation BS.

It was a feeding frenzy for the media, and conditioning to the minds of the ignorant and uninformed masses.

Days after the rally people were being arrested. Bank records were under surveillance for ATM transactions and local restaurants credit card charges in the DC Capitol area.

Street cameras were used to identify participants of the rally, not the riot.

They assumed everyone was automatically guilty of a crime because they attended the march. People were still in jail, years later, and their civil rights were being violated. https://www.reuters.com/world/us/us-judge-says-dc-jail-violated-civil-rights-jan-6-defendant-2021-10-13/

The media outlets in solidarity with Biden /Harris insisted this was an attack on Democracy, it was not. This lie was then repeated 24/7 on nightly news outlets for over two years.

The news media outlets, in my opinion are complicit in disseminating disinformation to Americans and must be held accountable.

If they had an iron clad case against Trump for saying "March peacefully toward the Capitol and let your voices be heard," they would not have put together the kangaroo court known as the January 6th Committee.

The committee consisted of mostly Democrats and some

Republican Trump haters. Republicans who had something to lose if Trump won. The committee would not release all of the Capitol Hill taped footage. No defense witnesses were called and they did not allow any questions from the opposing side.

This was a committee, not a trial, but people were sentenced with longer than usual jail time. Many believe their civil rights were ignored while incarcerated because the DC Warden Wanda Patten was a Democrat.

https://www.npr.org/2021/10/13/1045696978/judge-holds-washington-d-c-jail-officials-in-contempt-in-a-jan-6-riot-case

This was all because Democrats decided Trump was guilty of something the minute he came down the escalator in 2016.

Apples to Oranges

Now let's compare all that to the "summer of love," and the "mostly peaceful" BLM riots. We did not see a show of force when leftist protestors assaulted over sixty thousand police officers and over forty people were killed. They destroyed property, defaced statues, and injured many others. Police officers were fired if they fought back. It was absolute mayhem.

https://abcnews.go.com/US/60000-officers-assaulted-2020-31-sustaining-injuries-fbi/story?id=80661264

Very few were charged with crimes. In fact the protestors frequently sued for police brutality, using public defenders paid for by public tax dollars, unbelievable.

Anarchists rioted in January of 2017, on Trump's Inauguration Day but the media did not over report on it or hype it into an insurrection.

Rioters caused more damage across Washington DC to local businesses in January 2017 than occurred at the Capitol on January 6, 2021. Some anarchists carried signs that said, "No Borders, No Nations."

https://www.nbcnews.com/nightly-news/video/violent-anti-trump-protests-try-to-steal-spotlight-on-inauguration-day-859451971661

https://www.youtube.com/watch?v=SCu2gxVZ4E8

https://www.youtube.com/watch?v=cGUCq5fpMGo

Be as ready as you can be. This will afford you some extra peace of mind if times of trouble do come. Knowledge is also power.

I learned that each state has a National Guard, and some still have state militias as well, even some blue states.

The National Guard is activated by the state's Governor. It can also be activated by the President as Commander in Chief.

So why do you think Democrats continuously attempt to remove our Second Amendment rights? It's so we can't protect ourselves if the government decides to go rogue.

All Americans have the right to bear arms. If you don't want a gun, find something less lethal to protect your family in case of a civil unrest.

According to my research about 42% of American households own a firearm. While that is more than I expected, it is still not good enough.

https://www.statista.com/statistics/249740/percentage-of-households-in-the-united-states-owning-a-firearm/

Last, but certainly not least, let us remember to pray. God is good and He loves all of us the same.

As Christians we victoriously fight on our knees and God hears our sincere prayers.

I do believe America will obtain mercy, for now.

Americans have no problem with those who wish to come here legally, to assimilate, and become good Americans. This only makes America stronger.

But make no mistake, our future demographics may be changed forever.

When praying about this scenario I feel in the end we may be the future biblical "Babylon."

When I inquired what to do then, I was told….Shine your light in Babylon.

Pray for America, pray for Israel, pray the Lord delivers America from this evil time. Pray mercy so maybe the worst won't come upon us in the end.

Chapter Five

"America will never be destroyed from the outside. If we falter and lose our freedoms, it will be because we destroyed ourselves from within."

ABRAHAM LINCOLN

Education

Below are excerpts from my first book. I poured out my concerns and posed some solutions to turn the tide of the educational and moral decline in our nation.

America has lost her way in educational standards. From historically teaching in a local church which was the one room school house, to violent protests on college campuses, supporting terrorist propaganda fueled by foreign nationals and radical tenured professors.

Education, like mass media, is overwhelming in suggestive power. So it must be held to the highest of standards.

In chapter three, I brought forth the possibility we are all slowly being brainwashed by false narratives, misinformation, and disinformation. Extreme opposing views are dividing the nation.

These opposing forces, dare I say, are right versus wrong, left versus right, conservative versus liberal. When in reality it comes down to the basics. It's good versus evil. This is most true when it comes to our future and the next generation.

In 1925 the American Civil Liberties Union began its campaign against American values and morals by recruiting a football coach / substitute teacher disguised as a science teacher to intentionally teach evolution. This was to provoke a lawsuit for change, it was a first of many lawsuits to come. The Scopes Monkey trial succeeded to place the "Theory of Evolution" into the schools as a true science.
https://en.wikipedia.org/wiki/JohnT.Scopes

Today the same scientists who once backed evolution now have to pivot because advanced science can no longer support this flawed theory. Now the experts are saying we were seeded from other planets.

Six decades of students were taught this flawed science called Evolution. https://www.icr.org/article/3932
https://www.icr.org/article/8214

Even Darwin admitted he could not explain the complexities of human evolution;

Not to mention "…the missing link is still missing."

Since the 1960's the acknowledgement of God through prayer was removed from our school system.

For many years Republicans have promised to privatize public schools paid for by increasing tax dollars.

Privatizing public schools would benefit every student in every district and raise the level of success for all students. I laid out a simplified version of this possibility in my first book.

I also pointed out this has already been proven and is working better than the naysayers will admit. Below are some excerpts to explain why we need it throughout every city and state, so all neighborhoods will succeed.

Geoffrey Canada championed this effort in New York City. At first it was called Harlem Success Academy. Today it's called Promise Academy under the Harlem Children's Zone. It works, undisputed and should be a template for every big city, in every state.
https://hcz.org/
https://independentsector.org/people/geoffrey-canada/

This is the social justice issue everyone should be fighting for, instead of keeping the status quo. Where is the fight for equity in education? Real social equality starts with education reform from kindergarten to twelfth grade.

This provides real opportunity for success. This is the problem. It was always the problem, and it will continue to be the problem until something really big changes it.

"Privatizing education is the answer. It has already been proven to work, and the time to act is now."

Why don't We the People rise up and decide that a "Declaration of Education" is in order and demand that all schools be re-created equally for the 21st century?

All schools should be transformed into approved charter or privatized schools according to the needs of each community. They will all be funded with existing or perhaps less taxpayer dollars, as necessary.

This should include subsidizing parochial schools for up to half of the tuition costs to the benefit of the parents who support them and the students who attend.

They will be free from collective bargaining rights, union control and subject to quality teacher standards.

Employee retirement contributions and pay increases can be in line with what private sector professionals receive and negotiated with each individual school system.

Think of what a revolution this would be. Anyone with a heart for children knows this would be the right thing to do.
https://www.ted.com/talks/sir_ken_robinson_changing_education_paradigms?subtitle=en

This new educational alliance will encompass all existing public, specialty, charter, and private schools working together toward one common goal. To succeed in educating our children and raising the standards to reflect the best we have to offer.

Establish in each state an independent department of Charter, Specialty, and Private School Alliances Agency for general oversight. A committee streamlined to "enforce state laws that apply for top educational standards only."

Let the budget office calculate the overall cost savings of this proposal. How much can be saved if we eliminate all of the overlapping and unnecessary departments of education on the federal, state, and local levels nationwide.

How much can we save by using a web based curriculum or distance learning system for high performing students, used at home to reduce classroom size?

Subject programs can be updated electronically every year instead of printing every decade? Savings might be substantial enough to immediately and affordably implement several *go* systems.

First, use a self-paced curriculum for all the students currently being left behind. So students who are not currently performing at grade level can catch up at their own pace.

We should consider which teachers these students have had to root out the problems. I guarantee you will see a pattern form. There is so much that can be done to improve the quality of our schools.

First re-evaluate all curricula. Then implement block scheduling in all schools for all core subjects, English, Math, Science, and real American History. Especially including historic minorities who contributed to making America great; many of whom I did not learn about in my public school education.

Make minor facility or technology upgrades if necessary. Schools and parents can approve practical uniforms to implement a unified dress code. This is necessary to implement an equal footing of every student.

There should be plenty of revenue left over to compensate high quality teachers with more pay. Administrators can then decide reasonable increases in benefits based on ability, talent, and results, not merely the amount of time employed. Contract negotiations will be between the teacher's expectations and the employer's evaluations, without the need for outside union interventions.

Remove and defund all other special interests or extracurricular activities, regulatory bureaucracy, and enforcement related agencies.

Oversight can also be streamlined. Individual school meetings and or schools reports can be given by the existing administrators to the parents of all C/S/P students.

No more elected county school board members acting as mini politicians. Like those who were accusing concerned parents of being domestic terrorists.

Curriculum will be the best available and approved by each state for the C/S/P school. Whose members should have the highest standard of education. They must also represent the schools demographic and be free of political leanings and agendas.

The only agenda acceptable is educating the next generation to become world leaders in every field of study. Outside federal control won't be necessary. The school will answer directly to the community they serve. I believe parents will see better results within the first year.

C/S/P schools can individually construct the best system of teaching for their students. Or they could decide to

155

follow an existing charter or private school template and apply it accordingly.

Parents will show approval by virtue of enrollment. Reasonable transportation could still be provided through each individual school district.

Private transportation companies will compete for Charter /Specialized /Private schools individual contracts. Control, security, and oversight for C/S/P schools will be managed by each location just as private schools currently do.

Parents always reserve the right to take their funds or vouchers from the state and choose another charter, specialty, or private school suited to the needs of their children.

C/S/P schools would reserve the right to expect good behavior from all students conducive for a successful learning environment for everyone. Any student who does not comply will be dismissed and become the parent's responsibility to educate.

Parents who choose to home school should receive substantial reductions in their property taxes for absorbing the educational responsibility of their children.

Annual testing should still be required and encouraged to evaluate grade level proficiency of homeschooled students. So students can be supported up through graduation and beyond.

Senior residents who no longer have children in the school system should be exempt from paying the educational portion of their taxes.

Our historic Judeo Christian foundations should not be omitted or censored. Expressions of American traditions or our National holidays should be encouraged by name.

The demographics of a district may enjoy a holiday or celebration of their choosing. As long as it teaches Americanism first and is not prejudicial to America or Antisemitic.

Once the systems are upgraded and in place there will be no need for constant federal or state oversight or bureaucracy. The best systems usually run themselves.

The overall education should be world class and advanced, producing achievement levels this country has not seen in half a century. And we're going to need it because our international counterparts have been outperforming us for years.

Even though more money is spent on education every year, our children are barely learning the basics. They are deliberately being dumbed down, globalized, and greened. High school students are also being confused as to their own gender.

Activists are welcomed into today's public education system for what some would call indoctrination in the name of tolerance.

They target vulnerable kids at an age when they're already confused. The so-called experts know this, and I submit to you this is done purposefully.

This is all part of undermining our society by undermining basic cultural and moral standards held by families for generations. Today public education is one big social experiment.

Far left socialist liberals and special interest groups have targeted the learning years in hopes of transforming America from the inside. They have already done irreversible damage.

Realities of College

We have the same problem with college as we have with the K to12 public education. More often than not it costs more than it's worth. Except now students are in debt for ten to fifteen years, paying for the four to six year degree they earned and hoping it will help them earn a decent salary. Inaugural Gall the Audacity of Liberals by Lara Mars©2012

As parents we prep our kids for all the tests; the PSAT, the SAT, and the subject tests. Buying all the books and investing in prep courses for instruction. So your kid can get a great score, to apply to the best college, and earn a degree to qualify for the best paying job.

Then you work at that job, and hopefully it's something you like to do. Because you're well into your thirties before you pay off the loans, and that's if you didn't go to graduate school.

Isn't there a better way? We don't encourage individual entrepreneurship anymore. Immigrants came here from all over the world without any college at all. They opened stores and started businesses. They created wealth for themselves and jobs for other people by working hard, probably twelve to fourteen hours a day.

They were the shop keepers, shoemakers, bakery owners, and drycleaners. Legal Immigrants came here many without any college at all. Yet these legal immigrants were very successful and contributed to society through job creation and tax revenues to the government.

But hard work is often frowned upon and seen as grunt work especially to over educated elitists. Many in this generation don't want to work hard. They want to be paid well to do little or nothing.

Liberals often portray business owners and corporations as greedy, evil, and corrupt. Yet these companies provide the jobs we so desperately need.

Today parents sacrifice their children on the altar of a higher education for one of three reasons.

Either they believe it's the only way for their kids to have real success. They can't wait to ship them out and be free again. Or they believe they have failed as parents if they don't receive that acceptance letter.

It used to be only doctors and lawyers who needed college degrees. Now everyone has one which in my opinion makes you wonder what they are really worth, and some of the classes are extremely questionable.

Universities today are teaching as fact, flawed sciences like global warming and the "Theory of Evolution." Universities teach revised history or replace it with tolerance, diversity, and women's studies instead.

There is also the indoctrination of political correctness given to every college student on almost every college campus every day.

America's military is banned from some campuses while the dictator of Iran was welcomed to speak at a university in New York on behalf of world peace and knowledge through science.

Conservative speakers are heckled and practically assaulted and the students who share their conservative views must remain in their proverbial closet. Many of the classes today are also designed around the vision of a green and globally integrated world.

Excerpts from Inaugural Gall the Audacity of Liberals by Lara Mars©2012

College education today is little more than four more years of higher indoctrination. Universities today push a socialistic ideology designed to undermine Americas sovereignty, by pushing a socially just and globally green narrative in every facet of the college curriculum.

The real inconvenient truth here is that our college students are also being brainwashed into believing that the human race is ruining the planet, through excess carbon emissions and mass consumption. All this is based on the false teachings of global warming.

The colleges are perpetuating this hoax because of their socialistic alliances, and their support of the socialist union movements and the green global agenda.

Most disturbing is how our law colleges are teaching students to look to and depend on international law for insight, application, and interpretation of our laws, and not our US Constitution.

College students are also being encouraged to use violence and insurrection tactics as legitimate expressions of American tradition.

Teaching a united force should be used to solve economic, political, and social problems. Students are unknowingly being used for Antisemitic and Socialistic propaganda purposes.

Excerpts from Inaugural Gall the Audacity of Liberals by Lara Mars©2012

161

Why? So American born students will be compliant and accept a new lower standard of living in the United States in the name of social and environmental justice, fairness, and equity.

Opponents of this new lower standard will be labeled as greedy and insolent toward the needs of the rest of the world.

Capitalism v Socialism

Another lie being told to our college students is about Capitalism. Today it's said that Capitalism doesn't work.

But they are never taught about the horrors of Socialism, Communism, or Marxism. These systems of controlled government have left millions poor, destitute, or dead for opposing them.

Free market Capitalism is what made America great. It rewards everyone equally and does not discriminate. Success and prosperity can be had by all who dare to invest their money and sweat equity. If you are willing to take some risks, you can receive a larger return for your efforts.

Many people without advanced degrees have made their lives successful in America due to free market capitalism. Everyone has the same freedom to try, but we are never guaranteed the same outcomes.

And you don't need a college degree or years of college debt to achieve real success.

The second lie being told is that global warming is going to destroy the planet. I believe in what is called stewardship of the Earth. We are to take care of the planet, including animals, air, and waterways. We are not to worship the Earth or creation itself, but only the Creator.

The signs we see, in my opinion, are global warnings, not global warming.

It is unconscionable to rob these kids of the hope of their future. It's another attempt to control and deceive them into compliance.

Disinformation regurgitated by left leaning Socialist professors in a position of influence over their students must be stopped. They know full well they are over exaggerating cyclical weather patterns which repeat every hundred years or so.

This lie has been around since the 1970's. It started with Earth Day and has transformed into the biggest hoax perpetrated on this next generation.

Not to mention all the money being made from the UN to the green nonprofit hoaxers, who are taking billions of our tax dollars in what I call the green global scam.

Millions and millions of dollars are spent on remedial and higher education every year. The result of these investments should not be to indoctrinate, confuse, and lie to our young adults in order to destroy America from within.

Excerpts from Inaugural Gall the Audacity of Liberals by Lara Mars©2012

Devil's Advocate

I watched the testimony of Pamela S. Nadell during the committee hearing on antisemitism occurring on college campuses since Hamas attacked Israel on October 7, 2023. This was her opportunity to testify to the fact that colleges have been anti-Semitic for many years. She should have suggested any college participating in Anti-Israel, and Anti-American protests should be defunded immediately of public tax dollars.

I agreed with most of her testimony, until she said, "antisemites use code words like Globalists" and "participate in Soros bashing." That's where she lost me.

When Conservatives use the word Globalists they're not speaking about Jewish people in whole or in part. They are speaking of individuals who financially want to rule the world.

Globalists, in my opinion, are rich financiers of the world's economy, who are anti-god, and anti-national sovereignty.

They want to become rulers over everyone, controlling everything their money can buy. They want consolidation of the money and power in a global setting. So the few can rule over the many, while using global warming as their religious call to arms, and a crisis to unite the world.

I will speak against anyone who bets against or supports those who endanger America's existence. Against those who erase our history, or bankrupt our future, all enemies both foreign and domestic.

It was said George Soros promoted the McCain Feingold Act. This bill was passed in March 2002, and it gave birth to America's political action groups. This allowed Soros to funnel millions of dollars to influence America's elections. I believe Soros funds many political action committees, beginning with MoveOn.org, which was established after the Bush v. Gore election debacle in the year 2000.

Through these many super packs, and nonprofit organizations, he has become a major Democratic influencer. Soros is most likely part of the deep state, a shadow government that controls the new Socialist wing of the Democratic party.

He funded many of the "no bail" DA's and AG's across America, from New York City to Los Angeles, California.

The Progressives Soros funded enacted "no bail" policies, which released criminals and repeat offenders, and criminal illegals back on the streets. https://www.heritage.org/crime-and-justice/commentary/george-soross-prosecutors-wage-war-law-and-order

I believe these issues are all connected with a single purpose in mind. To undermine America's safety, security and ultimately to cause our demise through moral decay and anarchy.

Mr. Soros supports many non-profit organizations through his Open Society Institute. OSI receives many private and corporate donations. They also receive grant funds and monies from government sources like USAID and are not taxed because it is considered a nonprofit agency. In general non-profits are not compelled by law to disclose their donor information.

Most of the organizations he supports begin with the word "American." But their purpose is not necessarily to help America. Here are just a few organizations he supports...

https://www.drugfree.org.au/images/pdf-files/library/soros/2019/Organizations%20Funded%20Di

rectly%20by%20George%20Soros%20and%20his%20O
pen%20Society%20Institute2015.pdf

America Votes: Soros also played a major role in creating this group, whose get-out-the vote campaigns targeted likely Democratic voters.

America Coming Together: Soros played a major role in creating this group, whose purpose was to coordinate and organize pro-Democrat voter-mobilization programs.

American Bar Association Commission on Immigration Policy: This organization "opposes laws that require employers and persons providing education, health care, or other social services to verify citizenship or immigration status."

Alliance for Justice: Best known for its activism vis a vis the appointment of federal judges. This group consistently depicts Republican judicial nominees as "extremists."

American Family Voices: This group creates and coordinates media campaigns charging Republicans with wrongdoing.

American Friends Service Committee: This group views the United States as the principal cause of human suffering around the world. As such, it favors America's unilateral disarmament, the dissolution of American borders, amnesty for illegal aliens, the abolition of the death penalty, and the repeal of the Patriot Act.

American Federation of Teachers: After longtime AFT President Albert Shanker died in 1997, he was succeeded by Sandra Feldman, who slowly "re-branded" the union, allying it with some of the most powerful left-wing elements of the New Labor Movement.

American Constitution Society for Law and Policy: This Washington, DC-based think tank seeks to move American jurisprudence to the left by recruiting, indoctrinating, and mobilizing young law students, helping them acquire positions of power. It also provides leftist Democrats with a bully pulpit from which to denounce their political adversaries.

America's Voice: This open-borders group seeks to promote "comprehensive" immigration reform that includes a robust agenda in favor of amnesty for illegal aliens.

American Immigration Council: This non-profit organization is a prominent member of the open-borders lobby. It advocates expanded rights and amnesty for illegal aliens residing in the U.S.

American Immigration Law Foundation: This group supports amnesty for illegal aliens, on whose behalf it litigates against the U.S. government.

American Independent News Network: This organization promotes "impact journalism" that advocates progressive change.

The American Prospect, Inc.: This corporation trains and mentors young leftwing journalists and organizes strategy meetings for leftist leaders.

Amnesty International: This organization directs a grossly disproportionate share of its criticism for human rights violations at the United States and Israel.

Applied Research Center: Viewing the United States as a nation where *structural racism* is "deeply embedded in the fabric of society," ARC seeks to "build a fair and equal society" by demanding "concrete change from our most powerful institutions."

American Bridge 21st Century: This Super PAC conducts opposition research designed to help Democratic political candidates defeat their Republican foes.

American Institute for Social Justice: AISJ's goal is to produce skilled community organizers who can transform poor communities by agitating for increased government spending on city services, drug interdiction, crime prevention, housing, public-sector jobs, access to healthcare, and public schools.

Arab American Institute Foundation: The Arab American Institute denounces the purportedly widespread civil liberties violations directed against Arab Americans in the post 9/11 period and characterizes Israel as a brutal oppressor of the Palestinian people.

https://www.drugfree.org.au/images/pdf-files/library/soros/2019/Organizations%20Funded%20Drectly%20by%20George%20Soros%20and%20his%20Open%20Society%20Institute2015.pdf

We also need to return the non-profit status to legitimate religious organizations ONLY.

No more tax free dollars for anti-American radicals, not just Soros, but many others connected to radical unions and foreign entities.

This includes removing the non-profit status from the green and global nonprofits which produce nothing while receiving huge grant funding from American taxpayers amounting to millions and millions of dollars.

https://energyfundsforall.org/find-funding-for/nonprofits/

Education reform is the key to equality for every American child and young adult. This is imperative for the rebirth of America and to ensure our future success.

America needs an educational system that teaches and prepares our children to love this country and to lead in the 21st century.

My Father earned a PhD in law and served in the military all of his life. First in active duty during WWII, then in the Army Reserve for more than thirty years.

He retired as a Lieutenant Colonel, and his example caused me to love my country; and to this day I would lay down my life for America without hesitation.

Chapter Six

I have set watchmen on your walls, O Jerusalem;
They shall never hold their peace day or night.

Isaiah 62:6

<u>Watchman on the Wall</u>

"That is God's call for Israel, as well as all the nations;
To become watchmen on His walls, to watch, be alert,
keep vigil and be prepared for what is coming."

https://www.beithallel-israel.org/video/assuming-your-calling-as-watchmen-on-the-walls-of-jerusalem/#:~:text=They%20were%20the%20guards%20and,Israel%

Over a decade ago I wrote about several concerns. I attempted to explain about the Obama "change." Not a change for the better, but a shift that would inevitably corrupt government agencies, redistribute our wealth, and cause America to slowly decline.

We were warned Obama was a Socialist. That he was going to carelessly redistribute the wealth of America through the UN and around the world.

Several people sounded the alarm, but many Americans ignored the warnings. I believe it's time for another change hopefully causing a rebirth for America.

God is Speaking Are You Listening?

Scripture says in Genesis "Let the sun and moon be for signs and seasons" Gen 1:14

Signs were interpreted as warnings and seasons referred to God's appointed feast days for the Jewish people.

I believe God's calendar is the Jewish calendar. Not the Roman calendar we use that was changed by Julius Ceasar in 46 BC to a 365 day solar year with leap years every four years.

Although the Roman calendar was used during the life of Jesus Christ, Jesus himself abided by the Jewish calendar and kept the appointed feasts while fulfilling prophesy.

Jim Staley of Passion For Truth Ministries said "the Romans gave us holidays. The Creator gave us holy days." The holy days are set to specific lunar timelines.

The holidays coincide with the Summer /Winter solstice and are steeped in paganism.
https://www.youtube.com/watch?v=3_mcNX99VaU

God gave appointed feast days for His people to remember all His miracles, and to meet with Him for feasting, rest, and celebration. The sun and moon have been used by God throughout the generations to speak to and meet with His people.

Let's take a closer look at this, albeit an overview of what I believe is paramount for America to know in the near future. In an effort to persuade you that these happenings are not mere coincidences.

Just like "The Harbingers" revealed by author Jonathan Cahn have been consistent and eventful. The blood moons and total solar eclipses have meaning and purpose. Each with implications of wars, plagues, and rebirth of nations.

I will mention different names of various types of moons and eclipses in this chapter, and it can be confusing. So below are some meanings to clarify the differences.

Blood Moon- Is a total lunar eclipse that occurs when the Earth, Moon, and Sun are aligned during a full moon.

The moon appears red in a total lunar eclipse because of the Earth's shadow.

Tetrad Blood Moon- Is a specific type of blood moon that is a series of four total lunar eclipses within a two year period. Separated by six months and no partial eclipses in between. They are very rare.

Partial Lunar Eclipse- Happens when the Earth, Moon, and Sun are not aligned, causing the Moon to pass through only a part of the Earth's shadow.

Total Solar Eclipse- When the Moon passes between the Earth and the Sun completely blocking the face of the Sun.

Annular Solar Eclipse- Happens when the Moon passes between the Sun and the Earth but doesn't cover the Sun completely.

Partial Solar Eclipse- Happens when the Moon passes between the Earth and the Sun but the three are not in perfect alignment.

I watched Jim Staley's YouTube video prior to the total Solar Eclipse of 2024. I viewed it several times before I realized the tremendous implications for America.

The video simply explained events that have happened in the past and proposed events that may happen in the near future.
https://www.youtube.com/watch?v=3_mcNX99VaU

With Meaning and Purpose

Many blood moons and Tetrad blood moons appeared on Nisan I, the first month of the Jewish New Year. Many significant events for Israel have taken place on Nisan I throughout Jewish history.

For example, it was on Nisan I that Nehemiah returned to Jerusalem to rebuild the wall. About two years later on Nisan I, Ezra lead a group from Babylon to Jerusalem to reestablish the temple system. It is also believed that on Nisan I that Jesus was water baptized by John the Baptist and began to "build" His ministry and His kingdom to come.
https://www.youtube.com/watch?v=3_mcNX99VaU

According to Jewish and American history it was on Nisan I that Spain expelled the Jewish people, aka The Spanish Inquisition. At that exact time Christopher

Columbus set sail to America. Many believe the expelled Jews bought passage and helped financed that voyage to come to America. I encourage you to view the video and decide for yourself.

https://www.youtube.com/watch?v=3_mcNX99VaU

While explaining the relevance of the Tetrad blood moons some of the events mentioned in the video that coincided with blood moons were as follows...

162 AD – Roman War with the Parthians

795 AD – The Saxon War began

1492 AD – The Spanish Inquisition, when Spain declared war on, and expelled the Jewish people

1948 AD Israel became a reestablished nation. Israel was already recorded as a nation during biblical times.

1967 AD – Israel took back its ancestral capital Jerusalem, after being attacked by Egypt, Jordan, and Syria during the Six Day War. On June 5th to June 10th, 1967.

https://www.youtube.com/watch?v=3_mcNX99VaU

What About In America?

First let's look at some of the past total solar eclipses in America all bringing a warning of war, rebirth, and pestilence.

https://www.youtube.com/watch?v=3_mcNX99VaU

Before the 2017 total solar eclipse; America had a total solar eclipse on November 30, 1776. This was the last total solar eclipse to remain completely in the United States. It passed through 13 states beginning in Oregon and exiting through South Carolina. It was followed by a lunar eclipse two weeks later on December 15, 1776. https://www.eclipsewise.com/solar/SEprime/-1799--1700/SE-1776Nov30Tprime.html

Earlier that year on July 4, 1776, our Founding Fathers signed their names and adopted the Declaration of Independence declaring commitment to our sovereign independence from Great Britian.

We fought for our independence and won the **Revolutionary War which began on April 19, 1775, and ended on September 3, 1783**.

In the 1800's there was a solar eclipse on September 17, 1811. It was a relatively long annular solar eclipse according to eclipsewise.com.

On February 7, 1812, there was a massive earthquake, along the New Madrid fault line. It was so powerful that it caused the Mississippi River to flow backwards and it rang the Liberty Bell in Pennsylvania. https://www.youtube.com/watch?v=3_mcNX99VaU

A few months later on June 18 the War of 1812 began. It was again between America and Great Britian. This time for territory, not for our independence.

There was another Annular solar eclipse in 1831, after which America suffered three waves of a cholera epidemic that lasted from 1832 to 1866. It was caused from refugees fleeing the epidemic in the Caribbean.

In the early 1900's the year with the most solar eclipses was 1935. (wikipedia.org) In the 20th Century we had WWI, and WWII, then the Korean War followed by the Vietnam War, with too many events to list, we will fast forward to Y2K.

In America on January 21, 2000, there was a total lunar eclipse which is **considered a blood moon**. It was visible across the entire US. Then there was another on July 16, 2000, which was **also considered a blood moon**.

On September 11, 2001, America was hit by a terrorist attack. Using commercial airplanes the terrorists brought down the World Trade Center Twin Towers in New York City as we watched in disbelief.

Over three thousand Americans died in one day at the hands of nineteen terrorists. Terrorists who we allowed into this country because we were presumptuous and too trusting.

Everyone knows someone who was affected by this attack. We lost loved ones, and we vowed to never forget. This event changed America forever.
We immediately entered into a twenty year war in Afghanistan. Many believe it should not have taken that long. But America has too many government and non-government agencies interested in ongoing warfare.

Were the blood moons a warning? I believe they were. At the time I had not heard about their existence. Now America has been warned, and now we know what to look for so maybe we can be better prepared.

In the not so distant past there were four Tetrad blood moons occurring from April 15, 2014, to Sept 28, 2015.

Each landing on a specific Jewish holy day with a total solar eclipse in the middle (on Nisan I) on March 20, 2015.

The Tetrad Blood Moons, and one total Solar eclipse appeared in the heavens as follows….

April 15, 2014 – On the Jewish holy day of Passover / Blood Moon

October 8, 2014- On the Jewish holy days of Sukkot /
Blood Moon
March 20, 2015- ADAR 29 on Nisan I (total solar
eclipse)

April 4, 2015 – Jewish holy day of Passover / Blood
Moon

September 28, 2015- Jewish holy days of Sukkot / Blood
Moon

**Let's be clear only God can control and display
heavenly signs and events with flawless accuracy.**

In 2015, I believe the heavens posted these significant
Tetrad Blood moons and the solar eclipse as a warning
for Israel and the world.

Because it was <u>on July 14, 2015, then President Obama
entered into the controversial nuclear deal with Iran.</u>
With the promise that Iran would reduce their uranium
stockpile, Obama put Israel, the Middle East, and the
entire world in grave danger.

To this day Iran seeks nuclear capability with the
promise to wipe Israel off the map. As it continues to
finance terrorist groups to fight against Israel.

Namely Hamas in Gaza, the Houti's in Yemen, and Hezbollah, in Lebanon. To name just a few.

The Biden / Harris administration has provided Iran with billions of dollars and has followed Obama's soft on Iran policies by lifting the sanctions imposed by the previous Trump administration.

Afterwards, as cover, Biden said the money would be used for humanitarian purposes. Then Iran's leaders responded loud and clear that they will spend the money however they want.
https://nypost.com/2023/09/12/iranian-president-plans-use-the-6b-prisoner-cash-wherever-we-need-it/

Shortly after the money was released, Iran began to finance the deadly attacks against Israel by Hamas, Hezbollah and others declaring a war by perpetrating a massacre that started on October 7, 2023.

A Reason for Hope

The total solar eclipse on April 8, 2024, was more than a once in a lifetime rare celestial event for America. I believe the heavens were telling us something.

At first I was distressed, because let's face it America's leaders have really screwed up badly, especially when it comes to Israel.

First let's look back to August 21, 2017. For the first time in our lives a total solar eclipse crossed the continental US in a remarkable way.

Beginning in Salem Oregon, the path traveled through a total of fourteen states before exiting South Carolina.

What made it remarkable was the path crossed through seven cities named Salem.

https://www.youtube.com/watch?v=3_mcNX99VaU

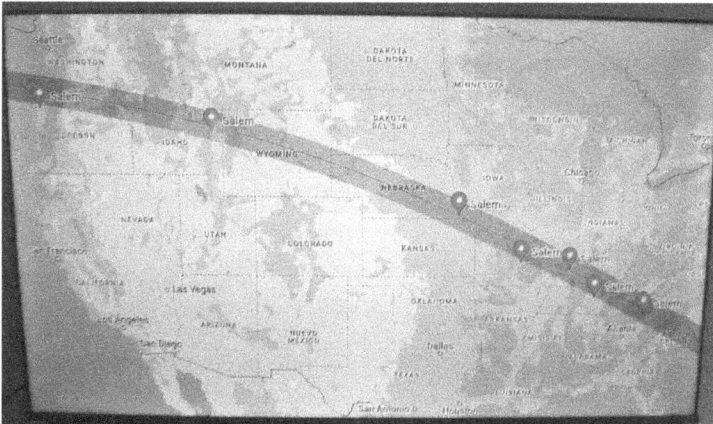

In Genesis 14, the City of Jerusalem was originally named Salem at the time when Abraham entered into Canaan around 2000 BC.

Salem is also mentioned in Genesis 14:18 when Abraham met Melchizedek, the King of Salem.

He was described as the Priest of the God Most High who gave bread and wine to Abraham.

This is a significant picture of the presence of Jesus in the Old Testament. In the New Testament Jesus is the symbol of Bread and Wine in Communion, as He confirmed at the Last Supper.

Now the total eclipse of April 8, 2024, was just as significant and amazing. Coming up from Mexico, the path of the eclipse first passed through Jonah, Texas, before it passed a total of six cities named Nineveh.

The first in Nineveh, Texas, then proceeded to pass directly through two more cities name Nineveh and passed close by four others.

In summation, the total of cities named Nineveh were as follows…Nineveh, Texas, Nineveh, Indianna, Nineveh, Ohio, Nineveh, Pennsylvania, Nineveh, New York, and Nineveh, Nova Scotia.

In the Bible, the prophet Jonah was sent to preach repentance to Nineveh or else they would be destroyed. Even though Jonah resisted, he went, and the wicked city repented and was spared of Gods judgement.

If you lay the April 8, 2024, eclipse path over the 2017 eclipse path it forms an X in Southern Illinois.
The X falls out in the middle of nowhere on a road named Salem Road.
https://www.youtube.com/watch?v=3_mcNX99VaU

After the Total solar eclipse in April 2024, we began hearing fearful voices talking about an earthquake along the New Madrid fault. Near where the X marked the spot. This was more than possible, many felt it was inevitable.

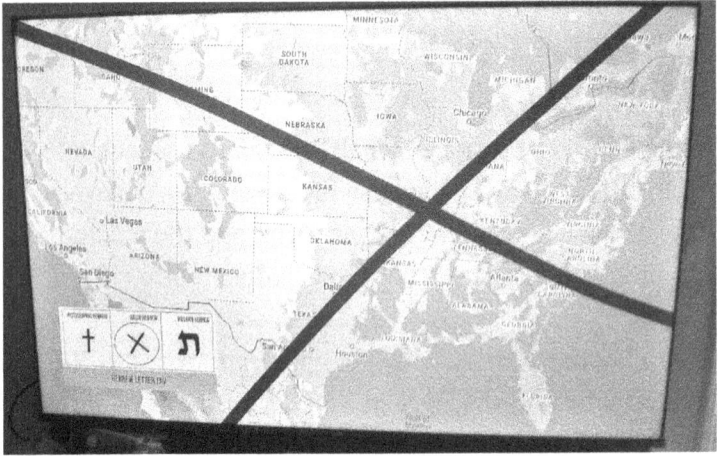

The speaker Jim Staley goes on to say the X formed the Hebrew letter Tov. In its earliest form it was the shape of an X or a cross. The pictogram symbol behind the shape of the letter tav is a mark or seal.

Could it be said the God of Heaven placed his mark or seal over America. But was it a mark of judgement or mercy?

https://www.youtube.com/watch?v=3_mcNX99VaU

After the horrific October 7, 2023, attack by Hamas on Israel, Americans immediately began to financially give, earnestly pray, and travel as volunteers to support missions and help Israel anyway they could.

The support continues to this day. I believe this brought a great mercy upon America.

Because exactly one week later on October 14, 2023, there was, in fact, another Annular solar eclipse. Though less prominent, many may not have heard about. It passed through seven states.

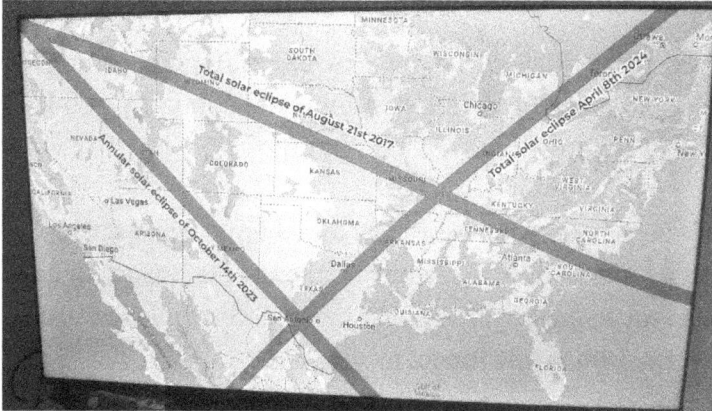

Beginning in Oregon, then Idaho, Nevada, Utah, Northeast Arizona, New Mexico, and Texas before exiting the US.

When you include this solar eclipses' path beginning in Oregon, and leaving through Texas, with the other two eclipses, it forms what the speaker called Aleph,

the first letter of the Hebrew alphabet.
https://en.wikipedia.org/wiki/Aleph

According to Wikipedia.org the original pictograph for Aleph represents an ox, strength, and means leader. It also represents the Oneness of God.
https://en.wikipedia.org/wiki/Aleph
https://hebrewtoday.com/alphabet/the-letter-alef-%d7%90/

According to an AI search, Tov has multiple meanings. It could mean beautiful, life giving, and morally good. It can also imply a fulfillment of purpose.

If you put the Aleph and Tov together it stands for seal or the Mark of Strength or Strength of the Leader. It can also mean the beginning and the end. Symbolic of Jesus as the Alpha and Omega in scriptures.

This is the "Mark" or seal God has placed over America. I believe we may now have mercy because of our immediate response of love, generosity, kindness, and overwhelming support to Israel in a time of great trouble.

If we do our part, accordingly the last total solar eclipse went specifically through Jonah, Texas, then the cities named Nineveh.

A Time of Renewal

It's not difficult to understand America…We must repent for our many wrongs, and I believe the God of Heaven will give America mercy.

Because the solar eclipses of 2017 and 2024 specifically named both Salem and Nineveh, in my opinion there is a specific message or meaning.

2 Chronicles 7:14-16 …"If my people, who are called by my name, will humble themselves and pray and seek my face and turn from their wicked ways, then I will hear from heaven, and I will forgive their sin and will heal their land."

I believe it's time for America to repent and change the way we operate personally, politically, and financially. We also need to apologize to our Creator for playing god in many ways. From the taking of innocent lives through abortions, to the making and funding of experimental viruses. And especially for funding ungodly dictators and so called democracies around the world.

Let's not discard the selfish creating of technologies designed to control humanity. Now expanding that control onto future generations.

Knowing eventually a godless global society will be worshipping this power of AI.

I am not suggesting we stop technology and go backwards. All things Written must come to pass. But we must control our selfish ambitions and be tempered with humility. While managing the knowledge of good and evil in the palms of our hands.

Remembering God gave us the wisdom to create things because He created us "In His Image."

Repent: A sincere admission of guilt for committing a wrong or for omitting to do the right thing. A promise to resolve not to repeat the offenses and make an attempt to reverse the harmful effects of the wrong.
https://en.wikipedia.org/wiki/Repentance#:~:text=Repen tance%20typically%20requires%20an%20admission,or %20the%20omission%20where%20possible.

Elections Have Consequences

The majority of Americans support Israel, and we do not want to support any of Israel's enemies. Yet our government agencies support the United Nations which uses their sub agencies like UNRWA and UNIFIL to give cover to and support terrorist activities under the guise of humanitarian aid.

Our government agencies and unelected State Aid departments must be overhauled to reflect our values and our standards. As well as the national goals of the tax paying American people.

Be advised, anyone who directly seeks harm against Israel or objects to America's support of Israel will be judged. Anyone who supports the enemies of Israel, supports a culture of death, and you will reap what you sow.

In the Near Future

Looking ahead there will be two blood moons visible in America appearing in 2025. There will also be two partial solar eclipses. One on March 29, 2025, and the second on September 21, 2025.

The first total lunar eclipse is on March 14, 2025, and will be visible across North America, South America, Hawaii, Western Africa, and far Western Europe.

Today all these areas are experiencing political turmoil. Or they are suffering under constant natural disasters.

The second total lunar eclipse will be on September 8, 2025. It will be visible in Asia, Australia, and eastern Africa. Rising over the rest of Africa and Europe and setting over eastern Asia and New Zealand. According to my research.

Tetrad blood moons are rare. **The next (set of four) Tetrad blood Moons won't be until 2032 / 2033** being flashed across the heavens as follows....

April 25, 2032, and October 18, 2032.
With a total Solar eclipse on March 30, 2033.
Then the last two Tetrad blood moons are April 14, 2033, and October 8, 2033.

According to the Roman calendar this will be the two thousand year anniversary of Christ's death and Resurrection. Many hope it will mark the end of this fallen world and usher in the return of Jesus Christ to the earth.

The End is Really the New Beginning

As I was watching a brilliant Millennial being interviewed by another, she was attempting to explain the financial earthquake she believed was coming soon.

One being a completely electronic, all-inclusive, encompassing the totality of your existence.

She explained "You're either all in, or according to the system you don't exist." She is right, although she did not address or understand the spiritual implications, only the physical and financial outcomes of this system on society.

When the time comes there will be a complete collapse of the current financial system. Then there will be takeover of commerce with electronic credits or digital dollars, which already exists. Paper or coin money will no longer have any value.

The timing will most likely be immediately following a catastrophic worldwide event.

I think it will be immediately following the Rapture or the "Catching Away" of the Church, the Bride of Christ as described in 1 Thessalonians 4:16-17.

Note the scripture Mathew 24:36 says "But concerning that day and hour no one knows, not the angels, nor the Son, but the Father only."

For the most part those who remain will be overwhelmed with fear and chaos. They won't care who or what makes the decisions that bring back some sense of stability and normalcy.

The Mark of the Beast will bring security to the next level. Everyone will receive a *mark* either on your hand or your head. Many believe this is a computer barcode within an implantable chip for humans.

We see it on everything. Soon it may be in everyone. This coincides with the medical implant I wrote about over a decade ago.

This is worth repeating......

It is Written:

They will all receive a "Mark" both great and small, rich, and poor...that no one may buy or sell unless they have the mark, or the name of the beast, or the number of his name.
New King James Version- Rev. 13:16

Authorities will need to know who is here, and who really vanished. An accurate account, not just people hiding or trying to escape their current financial responsibilities. So everyone will be subject to mandatory compliance.

The stage is set for a global compliance. We saw the intended divide of the vaccinated versus the unvaccinated.

How families were willing to abandon holidays and other family members because of all the fear disseminated by the complicit news and social media outlets.

Government agencies and most state leaders were compliant and or drunk on the power to control. Some had evil schemes to implement. Very few states stayed open, strong, and independent.

The post rapture state of the whole world will be far worse than we have ever seen. In my opinion the powers that be will say the missing were abducted by aliens. The media will back them up, with stories, and proofs of this false narrative.

Those who knew the missing will know better. Because they had been talking about it for many years. Movies were made; books were written. The gospel was preached around the world in many languages.

What Will You Believe

I believe the world's faith will be challenged at this time causing "the great falling away." (2 Thes 2:2-9 NKJV)

I also believe the world leaders will claim that archaeologists have found the body of Jesus Christ in an effort to debunk faith in His Resurrection.

This will be the news cycle 24/7 until most believe it to be true. This lie will be in full compliance with the new world leaders as ordered.

They will present false evidence, confirmed by the false experts, or a false prophet and DNA compared to (and most likely taken from) the Shroud of Turin, now said to be linked to Jesus Christ.
 https://www.newsmax.com/newsfront/jesus-blood-shroud/2024/09/05/id/1179195/

Hold fast to your faith, and do not believe them.

Remember first Christ removes His Bride the *church* in the Rapture. Then Christ removes the two Jewish witnesses in Jerusalem, in the book of Revelation.

Then He removes His "Elect," that is all the Jewish believers and all those who came to faith during the tribulation period. At the end of seven years, Jesus Christ will return again and He will establish a new Heaven and a new Earth.

All who love Him will be with Him forever......
He has given us proof, in both Old and New Testaments.
His Word is truth, and He always keeps His promises.

Alpha and Omega

The world's history both past and the future to come, was given to mankind in the book of Daniel Chapter 2:32. A king was disturbed by a dream he could not understand. Daniel asked God to reveal the dream and through this interpretation the kingdoms of the world to come were made known to mankind. Including the end of the ages.

God revealed the kingdoms of the earth and what would be from the Babylonian kingdom of gold (head) to the Roman Empire made of legs of iron. And the feet were a mix of iron and clay.

Many believe this is the state of the world today. Represented in the revised Roman Empire as the United European Union (iron) and mixed with man's vision (clay) through the agenda of the United Nations.

Then the feet are smashed by a Rock not made by human hands. The "Rock" is Jesus Christ. Which destroys it all and turns history into dust.

It then becomes the "Mountain of God." Which is His kingdom to come, and His will being done.

The bible says we should comfort one another with this truth. Jesus Christ will return for His own. How do you know if you belong to him?

Easy, If you're waiting for Him, He's coming for you

If you're not waiting for him, He's not coming for you.

But you can decide to change that today and to become a forgiven child of God. Yes, some things in your life may change, but mostly for the better. It's not hard, there's nothing you have to physically do.

Only confess and believe on the Lord Jesus Christ
Repeat the prayer below and then tell someone you did.
Maybe find a church for fellowship and support.
Hold on tight because He's coming soon.

Those who have ears let them hear...

If you would like to personally know the God of which I speak in this book. Please feel free to repeat this prayer.

As long as it is said from your heart with sincerity, He will hear you and He will answer.

Here are some promises to encourage your faith.

The Bible says in the book of Romans Chapter 10:9

That if you confess with your mouth, "Jesus is Lord," and believe in your heart that God raised him from the dead, you will be saved.

In 2 Corinthians 5:17

Therefore, if anyone is in Christ, he is a new creation; old things have passed away: behold, all things have become new.

In John 6:37 Jesus said…"All that the Father gives Me will come to Me, and the one who comes to me I will by no means not cast out."

You will never be rejected.

So standing on these, and many other biblical promises Jesus Christ made to all who believe in Him,

Please repeat this prayer….

Lord Jesus, I know that I am a sinner, and I am in need of your forgiveness.

I ask the Father in your name Jesus, to forgive me for all my sins and all my iniquities,

To wash me clean with the precious blood that You shed for me on the Cross at Calvary,

So I can be called a child of God. Redeemed by Your sacrifice and saved by grace.

Come into my heart right now and be my Lord and my Savior.

Fill me with your Holy Spirit, and guide me always, from this day forward until all Eternity,

in Your name, Lord Jesus I pray Amen.

In Conclusion

Pray America calls upon God for help.

Pray America stays faithful to help protect Israel.

Pray America is delivered from this dangerous time.

Pray Mercy for America and victory and peace for Israel.

May God bless you and keep you always :)

www.ingramcontent.com/pod-product-compliance
Lightning Source LLC
Chambersburg PA
CBHW022107280326
41933CB00007B/284